# HOW
# TO
# GET
# LUCKY

# HOW TO GET LUCKY

## MAX GUNTHER

STEIN AND DAY/Publishers/New York

First published in 1986
Copyright © 1986 by Max Gunther
All rights reserved, Stein and Day, Incorporated
Designed by Louis A. Ditizio
Printed in the United States of America
STEIN AND DAY/*Publishers*
Scarborough House
Briarcliff Manor, N.Y. 10510

**Library of Congress Cataloging-in-Publication Data**

Gunther, Max, 1927-
    How to get lucky.

    Includes index.
    1. Success.   2. Fortune.   I. Title.
BJ1611.2.G857      1986      158'.1          85-40245
ISBN 0-8128-3054-7

# CONTENTS

## PART I  THE COMMANDING FACTOR

## PART II  THE TECHNIQUES OF LUCKY POSITIONING

PART I

# The Commanding Factor

# 1. The Supreme Insult

William S. Hoffman was a gambler but not a successful one. He wrote a book about his life entitled *The Loser.* Trying to sort out the reasons why he was never able to make it, he arrived at a very interesting conclusion: *He failed because he tried to deny the role of luck in his life.*

He had learned this unproductive and dangerous attitude from his father, an athletic coach. The senior Hoffman liked to peptalk his teams with windy pronouncements derived from the Work Ethic. One of his favorites was: "If you're good, you don't need luck."

What nonsense.

*Of course* you need luck. It doesn't matter how good a football player you are. If you have the bad luck to trip on a loose stair runner and sprain your ankle the night before the big game, none of your hard-earned strengths and skills are going to do you the least bit of good. All those hours of practice, all that admirable grit and determination—all are down the drain. The coach can recite Work Ethic apothegms at you until he is blue in the face, but he cannot change the facts.

It isn't enough just to be good. You've got to be lucky, too.

The junior Hoffman, the gambler, evidently listened too seriously to his father's bad advice. He thought he could become a successful gambler through sheer hard work. All he had to do, young Hoffman believed, was apply himself to an assiduous study of horses, cards, or dice. "If you're good, you don't need luck." Having become good, he figured, he would be in a position to conquer the world.

That was what he thought. Things didn't work according to plan. Bad luck hit him. He wasn't prepared to handle it. He went broke.

You have *got* to have good luck. Without it, nothing will work right for you. Good luck is the essential basic component of success, no matter what your personal definition of "success" may be.

What is it you want from life? To be rich? Famous? Respected in a profession? Happily married? Well loved? Whatever your goals may be, have you achieved them? It is unlikely you would be reading this book if your answer were yes.

Nearly all of us would have to answer no, we have not yet achieved our goals. And why not? Apply the question to your own life. What is it that has prevented you from getting where you want to be? Is it that you aren't good enough? Or simply that you haven't been lucky enough?

The second answer—not lucky enough—is by far the more likely to be the truth. Most of us are "good" in one way or another—good enough, as often as not, to reach whatever goals we have wished to set for ourselves. We have failed to reach those goals largely because of a lack of luck.

There are any number of ways to demonstrate this truth to yourself. It was emphasized strongly for me during a recent period when, quite by chance, I went to see a series of plays performed by amateur theatrical groups in my home county. Many of the groups' members told me that they had dreamed of acting professionally but were still waiting for the big break—or had given up waiting. I asked myself why the big break had never come their way. Lack of talent? Certainly not, in most cases. These men and women were at least as good as the stars we see every week on TV or at the movies. What was the difference, then? Why had the stars soared to a pinnacle of success while thousands of other actors and actresses, equally good, were never able to climb higher than a hometown dramatic club?

There was only one answer: luck. Being in the right place at the right time. Knowing somebody who knew somebody.

## The Supreme Insult

Being good simply is not enough.

LUCK. IT BLUNDERS in and out of our lives, unbidden, unexpected, sometimes welcome and sometimes not. It plays a role in all our affairs, often the commanding role. No matter how carefully you design your life, you cannot know how that design will be changed by the working of random events. You can only know the events will occur. You can only wait for them and hope they are in your favor.

Luck is the supreme insult to human reason. You can't ignore it, yet you can't plan for it. Man's grandest and most meticulous designs will fail if they are hit with bad luck, but the silliest ventures will succeed with good luck. Misfortune is always striking good people who don't deserve it, while many a scoundrel dies rich and happy. Whenever we think we have some answers, luck is there to mock us.

Is there anything to be made of it? Anything sensible to be said of it? Anything useful to be done about it?

Surprisingly, yes, there is. Probably more than you think.

You cannot control your luck in a precise way. You cannot say, "I want the next card I draw to be the queen of diamonds," and have any reasonable expectation of that outcome. Luck isn't amenable to fine tuning of that kind. To hope for such control is to dream of magic. It doesn't happen.

But you *can* bring about a substantial and even startling improvement in the quality of your luck. You can turn it from mostly bad to mostly good, from pretty good to better. Wherever you need luck and have been seeking it—in investments, gambling, career, love, friendships—you can upgrade your chances of becoming one of life's winners.

I know this is true because I've seen it happen. The luck-changing precepts you are about to study—the thirteen techniques of lucky positioning—are not just wisps of gassy theory. They were not invented by a bearded shrink sitting in his study, puffing on his pipe. Instead, they are derived from direct observations of men's and women's lives.

The lucky and the unlucky: What are the differences between them? What do the lucky know, what do they *do,* that the unlucky don't? Are

**13**

they lucky because they have some special ways of handling life or because—well, just because they're lucky?

I've been pursuing the answers to these questions for more than twenty years.

# 2. The Factor Nobody Talks About

We had better define our term before we go further. So:

Luck (*noun*): Events that influence your life but are not of your making.

Such events—good luck and bad luck—are the main shaping forces of human life. If you believe you are in perfect control of your life, you are kidding yourself.

You owe your very existence to a chancy event that happened before you were born: the coming together of your mother and father. How did they first meet? You will almost certainly discover that it was by chance. Because of that random event, you are alive today. The random mixing of chromosomes dictated your sex, your size, the color of your skin and eyes, the shape of your nose, your predisposition to certain diseases, and a host of other factors that you had no control of; factors that have already influenced your life heavily and will go on influencing it until it ends.

Other lucky and unlucky events have occurred, or will occur, during your lifetime. Events such as winning a million-dollar lottery prize; getting killed in an air crash; falling into a golden career opportunity through somebody you meet at a party; contracting cancer; stumbling into a life-changing love affair through a mix-up in theater seats; losing

15

your shirt in a stock market crash. Events of this nature can profoundly affect your life but aren't of your making; and all of them, hence, fit our definition of "luck."

Luck is one of the most important elements in men's and women's lives. Indeed, in many lives it is unequivocally *the* most important. Yet, strangely, people don't talk about it much. In fact, most people are like William Hoffman, the gambler, and his father, the coach: They are reluctant to acknowledge luck's huge influence.

It will be useful to take a brief look at this reluctance. You must clear it out of your way before you can begin the process of changing your luck.

WHY DO PEOPLE deny the role of luck? For one thing, we hate to think we are at the mercy of random happenings. We prefer to stay snugly wrapped in the illusion that we control our own destinies.

Life seems safer when I can say to myself, "The future will happen as I plan it." It won't, of course. Deep inside, we all know it won't. But the truth is too scary to contemplate without an illusion to snuggle up against.

Another reason why we prefer not to discuss luck's role is that it diminishes us and steals our dignity. Go to your local library and pick up any stage or screen star's autobiography. How did this man or woman rise to such an exalted position? Why, by being smart, talented, courageous, and resolute, of course.

And lucky? You aren't likely to find the word mentioned.

What the star fails to emphasize is that he or she began the long climb in competition with thousands of other smart, talented young hopefuls. We don't know their names today because they didn't get the big break. Of all those deserving young aspirants, only one was lucky enough to be slinging hash in a diner when a great producer stepped in for a bowl of chili.

Though it is usually obvious to any astute reader that the star's success was largely a result of blind luck, the star naturally does not dwell on that fact. You will hardly ever find a movie autobiography that says, "I'm really just an ordinary clod. I'm no more beautiful, talented or resolute than all those competitors whose names you don't know. In fact a lot of them would look better on a movie screen than I do. The only thing they didn't have was luck." Such a confession would diminish the star's luminosity.

The reluctance to talk about luck isn't confined to the theatrical business, of course. All successful people avoid diminishment in the same way. Business executives do it in explaining how they got to be chairman of the board. Military officers do it in recalling how they won great battles. Politicians do it in listing the things that went right during their time in office. Luck, if mentioned at all, is never emphasized.

You will never see a president of the United States standing in front of a TV camera and saying, "Well, folks, nobody has the faintest idea of how it happened, but during my term at the White House, no new wars have broken out and the unemployment rate dropped. I'm one of the luckiest presidents you'll ever have!"

Nor will you ever hear a stock market speculator admit that his great killing, the one that made him rich, was the result of sheer luck. After the fact, he will construct a chain of reasoning to demonstrate how cleverly he figured everything out.

STILL OTHER REASONS for denying luck's role lie embedded at odd angles in the Work Ethic, also known as the Protestant or Puritan Ethic. We are taught from kindergarten on that we're supposed to make our way in life by hard work, perseverance, fortitude, and all those grindstony things. If, instead, we make it by blind luck, we're ashamed to say so in public—or even to admit it to ourselves.

Conversely, if we are walloped by bad luck, our Puritan heritage encourages us to think it's probably our own fault. We are supposedly responsible for our own outcomes, whether good or bad.

"Character is destiny," Heraclitus wrote some twenty-five centuries ago. Great stacks of plays, novels, movies, and TV dramas have since tried to prove the point. They haven't succeeded because it is unprovable. The best you can say of it is that, in some lives, it is half true. If I'm unlucky enough to be killed by a drunk driver on the highway, my destiny has nothing to do with my character. I might have been a saint or a sinner, a great philosopher or a bumbling nincompoop. None of that matters. My destiny has arrived. I'm dead.

Despite its obvious weakness, Heraclitus's aphorism survives, deeply embedded in our cultural consciousness. If things go wrong in your life, you aren't supposed to blame bad luck. Instead, you're supposed to look for the reasons inside yourself.

Those inside-the-self reasons may be pretty hard to find. Let's say you're unemployed. Why? Because the company you worked for went bankrupt. The debacle wasn't in any way your fault; it was just bad luck. But if you offer that as the reason for your jobless state, people will mutter behind your back that you are only whining or making excuses. They will suspect that the real reason for your joblessness is a personal flaw of some kind.

Or perhaps your hunt for a new job has been frustrated by prejudice based on race, ethnic origin, or age. That isn't your fault, either; it is just more bad luck. But if you say that's what it is, only a few will believe you.

We are culturally conditioned to deny the role of luck. The search for those elusive inside-the-self reasons even clouds our understanding of literature. All American and European kids (and for all I know, Russian and Chinese kids, too) get the "tragic flaw" theory of great literature laid on them in high school or college. This theory holds that in Shakespeare's tragedies or Dostoevski's novels or the epic poems of Homer, the heroes and heroines always bring their troubles on themselves through some failing of character. Teachers and professors insist that this is so, and many generations of kids have been given the same choice: agree or flunk.

The fact is, however, that you have to look pretty hard to find those "tragic flaws" that supposedly are behind the tragic happenings. There is no good evidence that either Homer or Shakespeare, for example, bought this goofy theory. In the *Iliad,* much of what happens is brought about by the manipulations of the gods—in other words, by good and bad luck that the human characters have no control of. Shakespeare's tragedies are similar. *Hamlet* opens with the hero in a fix because of events he had nothing to do with. It ends with nearly everybody dead by mistake—a blither of bloody blunders. It isn't a play about tragic flaws. It is a play about bad luck.

Why do English professors deny it? A good answer was offered recently by Phyllis Rose, a professor of English at Wesleyan University and no fan of the "tragic flaw" notion. Students are taught that the character flaw is a necessary ingredient of tragedy, Professor Rose wrote in *The New York Times*. "If the hero or heroine didn't have a flaw, it wouldn't be tragic because it wouldn't 'mean' anything. It would just be bad luck."

She added, wryly, "To convince students that bad luck isn't tragic must take some fancy teaching." But that is what is taught, and most people seem to buy the notion. And now, we have uncovered yet another reason why the role of luck in human experience is so persistently denied. Luck isn't "meaningful" enough. We yearn for life to have meaning. Acknowledging luck's role takes half the meaning out of it.

If I do wrong and come to a bad end as a direct result of my own wickedness or weakness, the episode is supposed to teach some kind of lesson to me and others. But if I'm peacefully walking along the street and get run over by a truck, nobody learns anything.

Life is like that much of the time: completely random and meaningless. Not only college English professors but all the rest of us are uncomfortable with that fact. But it is a fact you must look square in the eye if you want to do something about your luck.

The first step toward improving your luck is to acknowledge that it exists. That brings us to the First Technique of Lucky Positioning.

# PART II

# The Techniques of Lucky Positioning

What are the differences between the consistently lucky and the unlucky? Are there *reasons* why some men and women seem to get all the good breaks, while others get few or none?

The answers come from studies of more than one thousand adult lives. It turns out that lucky people characteristically organize their lives in such a way that they are *in position* to experience good luck and to avoid bad luck. There are thirteen principal ways in which the lucky do this. Not all of them practice the techniques consciously, and very few practice all thirteen. With most, it's six or eight techniques. But that is usually enough. If you look at the lives of the unlucky, by contrast, you may find two or three of the techniques in halfhearted use, but you are just as likely to find none in use.

If you want to improve your luck, study the thirteen techniques carefully. Not all the techniques may be immediately applicable in your particular case, but you will undoubtedly find you can apply some of them right away. Others can be held in reserve for the future.

Your life is about to change dramatically. Enjoy it.

# 3. The First Technique: Making the Luck/Planning Distinction

Paula Wellman is a veteran roulette croupier and "21" dealer. She has worked at several casinos in Las Vegas and Atlantic City. Occasionally, she gambles herself. She enjoys poker. But most of all, she says, she enjoys watching others gamble.

"I try to figure out what makes a winner or loser," she says. "Some people do a lot better than average over the long run and some do a lot worse. What makes the difference? I used to think nothing did—I mean there was no explanation that made any sense; it was just the breaks. But when you watch as many winners and losers as I've seen over the years, you begin to see some differences in the personalities."

What differences?

"Here's one thing that stands out. When a loser loses, it's because his luck was bad. When he wins, it's because he was smart."

We have arrived at the first great truth of luck control. If you want to be a winner, you must stay keenly aware of the role luck plays in your life. When a desired outcome is brought about by luck, you must acknowledge that fact. Don't try to tell yourself the outcome came about because you were smart. *Never* confuse luck with planning. If you do that, you all but guarantee that your luck, in the long run, will be bad.

Paula Wellman tells a story to illustrate the truth.

23

[It should be emphasized here that this isn't a book about casino gambling. It is about luck in all areas of human life. However, you will find gambling mentioned quite often, and the reason is this: Around the casinos, truths about luck are illustrated in a peculiarly stark, clear way. For the same reason, you will also find that the book contains many stories about the stock market and other great casinos where people deal daily with the distilled essence of luck. The book will make you a better casino gambler or stock market plunger if that is what you wish, but that is not its specific purpose. It is designed to make you luckier in *any* area of your life in which you need luck or have been seeking it. The Atlantic City and Wall Street stories are here only because they illustrate important points with such lovely clarity.]

Paula Wellman's story deals with a woman who came to Atlantic City to play roulette. She was a high school teacher, aged about forty, divorced and unrich. She thought she might supplement her teacher's salary by betting on the wheel. She had a *system.*

The idea of an infallible system for beating the wheel has engaged gamblers' attention for centuries. René Descartes devised a system in the seventeenth century and applied it to roulettelike games that were popular in those days in Paris and Amsterdam. He was too much of a skeptic to take the system seriously, and he quickly abandoned it when he saw that it could not work reliably. But thousands of other, less clever gamblers—millions, perhaps—have pinned their hopes on systems of various kinds; and most of them, in the long run, have regretted it.

If it were possible to devise a roulette winning system that really worked, you can be perfectly sure the world's casinos would have learned about it long ago and would have changed the rules of play so as to make it inoperable. The casinos do encourage the myth that such systems are possible, for that lures suckers and their money. People believe what they want to believe. If you believe you can outthink the wheel, you can buy all kinds of "secret formulas" and other advice in the streets and bars of any gambling town.

Some roulette systems are based on occult phenomena: lucky

numbers, astrological forces, and so on. Some depend on scientific-sounding rules, such as "the maturity of the chances," by which you are supposedly able to get advance information about the order in which random numbers will come up. Paula Wellman's teacher friend rejected both those approaches as fallacious. She had something better. Or so she thought.

What she had was a system that governed when and how much she should bet. She thought she had invented it. In fact, roulette betting systems (also applicable to a lot of other gambling games) have been around since Descartes's day. They go by romantic-sounding names such as the Martingale and the D'Alembert. Though they differ in detail, all of them rest essentially on the idea of increasing the sizes of your bets so as to recoup previous losses. Thus, if you're down by ten dollars, you bet enough so that a win, if it occurs, will bring you back your ten dollars plus the amount of the new bet. If you lose again, you bet a still larger amount the next time around. And so on, with variations.

Foolproof, right? Yes, it does have that sound. The Martingale and the D'Alembert and their many cousins do seem alluringly logical when you first learn about them or re-invent them. You may scoff at astrology, and your good natural skepticism may make you wary of pseudoscientific notions about the maturity of the chances, but a construct like the Martingale betting system may appeal to you strongly. It seems so sensible.

Thus it was with Paula Wellman's teacher friend. The very fact that she could reject astrology and other unscientific ideas gave her a special kind of confidence in herself. "I'm obviously not a gullible fool," she could say with satisfaction. "I've got a brain and I use it. I won't buy just anything."

However, the problem with Martingale-style betting systems is that they ignore two factors that turn out to be much more important than they seem. One is what gamblers call "strain," meaning the demand placed on gambling capital while one is waiting for a win. The other is the fact that all casinos place strict limits on the sizes of permissible bets at each table.

The Martingale system will work tolerably well as long as you aren't subjected to a longer-than-average string of consecutive losses. When such a string occurs—as it must, sooner or later—the system collapses.

Or to put it another way: *The system works when you are lucky.*

A Martingale-style betting system, therefore, is not that different from systems based on astrology, lucky numbers, dream interpretations, the maturity of the chances, or omens read in tea leaves. *All* will work or appear to work sometimes—when you are lucky.

Paula Wellman's teacher friend applied her system at the wheel one night and was lucky. She won. Unfortunately for her, she did not understand clearly *why* she had won. She believed it was because of her system.

She tested the system again on the following day and won again. And as before, she gave credit to the system instead of to luck. She began to think the system might be infallible.

Full of confidence, she withdrew a large amount of new gambling capital from her savings account. She took the money to a wheel where she could play for high stakes and lost every dime.

She was astounded. How could an infallible system fail?

It took her a long time to understand what had happened to her. The system had never really worked at all. It was certainly not infallible. Her early wins had been generated by luck, and finally, that good luck had run out. It was that simple—and, because she did not understand it at the time, it was that disastrous.

We will return later to the phenomenon of streaks and runs of luck; a phenomenon so puzzling and so desperately important in human life that we will need to consider it from several different angles. For now, the point to be appreciated is that every run of luck *must* end sooner or later. This is sad but not necessarily dangerous. When you enjoy a winning streak, you are safe as long as you see clearly what part of it was brought about by planning and what part by luck. The roulette-playing teacher strayed into danger when she ignored the role of luck. She thought her winning streak was strictly the result of planning. Believing that, she was not prepared for the streak to end.

The same kind of disaster befalls investors and speculators around Wall Street every day. Typical sad story: An investor comes into the market with a *system,* more than likely picked up from one of hundreds of newsletters and advisory services that are hawked in publications like the *Wall Street Journal.* For a couple of months or maybe a year or two, the system seems to work. The investor gets richer. "Hey, wow!" he exults. "I've found the secret! How smart I am!"

That is a dangerous thing to think. For the truth is that this super system has been working only because the investor has been lucky. In time, that good luck is bound to run out; but the investor refuses to consider such a possibility. Believing himself to be winning because of his superior intellect, he speculates less and less cautiously. Finally— *crash!*—his house of cards collapses around his ears.

And it doesn't happen only to individual men and women or only to beginners. It happens to the big boys, too. All of them are at the mercy of luck, and most of them refuse to admit it.

Take Standard and Poor's Corporation as an example. S&P is one of the oldest and most respected names in and around the Street. It publishes a weekly newsletter of investment advice called *The Outlook,* in which it says what its experts believe will happen on the stock market in months ahead. Subscribers are told what stocks they should buy and sell, when and why. The advice sounds very solemn and sensible. S&P itself often seems to lose sight of the fact that the rightness of its predictions is determined to a large extent by luck; and if S&P forgets that, undoubtedly many of the subscribers do too, particularly the newer ones.

S&P was unlucky in 1984. In January of that year *The Outlook* forecast that the S&P 500-stocks index (one of the Street's most widely followed indexes of stock prices) would end 1984 "more than 20% above the current level." The guess was grossly overoptimistic. What actually happened was that the S&P 500 index finished the year virtually unchanged, while other big indexes such as the Dow dropped a bit. For most investors, it was a so-so year to own stocks. Contrary to S&P's glowing prediction in January, you would have been better off keeping your money in a savings bank—or a pillowcase.

Did the bad forecast indicate that S&P was dumb? No, just unlucky. What *was* dumb was to leave luck out of the forecast. It should have been worded so as to make it plain that luck played as big a role in its outcome as analytical thinking. "We believe," it should have said, "that if we are lucky, the S&P 500 index will end the year up 20%."

S&P did not promise, of course, that its forecast would turn out right. Under the Securities & Exchange Commission's rules, financial advisers are forbidden to make guarantees. Even if they have enjoyed a string of lucky hits, they are required by law to warn subscribers that past successes may not be repeated in the future. But such warnings are never emphasized enough. The emphasis is always on the analytical thinking, not the luck. A subscriber, particularly a neophyte, can too easily be lulled into a sense of security that is entirely without foundation. "Oh boy!" the new investor thinks. "S&P says the market will go up 20 percent this year! This S&P is a company loaded with veteran financial thinkers. If *they* say something will happen, I can count on it!"

So the investor puts his or her life savings into the stock market. Bad luck intrudes, and everybody goes down the drain.

What new investors don't realize and even veteran investors forget is that bad luck can as easily strike the Street's greatest analysts as anybody else. It doesn't matter how astute S&P's thinkers may be or how many Harvard Business School degrees they may boast. Bad luck can hit them as readily as it hits you or me.

If you want further proof of this, look at Wall Street's mutual funds. In case you aren't familiar with them, a mutual fund is essentially a public money pool, designed especially to help new and inexperienced investors reap the alleged benefits of stock and bond ownership. If you have a little wad of capital and lack the experience, the confidence, or the time to play with it yourself, you buy shares in a mutual fund. The fund's managers then invest your money for you. You pay for the service, of course.

What do you get in return? Well, here's the sales pitch: You get high-powered investment thinking, the fund's sales brochure will tell you. Instead of floundering about in the market on your own, you put your financial well-being in the hands of Wall Street veterans who will always know the best thing to do.

The brochure and the honey-voiced saleswoman who phones you will make it sound like very nearly a sure thing. How can you lose? If these high-powered fund people can't make money on the market, nobody can!

Or so they try to tell you. What the brochure and the saleswoman don't say is that these vaunted financial thinkers are fully at the mercy of luck. It won't matter how carefully and with what marvelous logic they plan your financial future. If luck turns against them, you will lose your money just as easily as if you were blundering around on your own.

Turning back to the gloomy year 1984 for some examples, let's see how you would have fared if you had bought mutual fund shares that January. It would have depended, of course, on luck. Some fund managers (and their shareholders) were lucky in 1984, while others weren't.

The luckiest were the managers and shareholders of the Prudential-Bache Utilities Fund, which, as its name says, concentrates on investments in public-utility securities. According to Lipper Analytical Services, which monitors fund performances every year, Prudential-Bache won the 1984 sweepstakes with a very respectable gain of 38.6 percent. For every dollar you might have put into this fund at the beginning of 1984. you would have ended the year with nearly $1.40.

The unluckiest shareholders, according to Lipper's tabulation, were those of the 44 Wall Street Fund, which specializes in more speculative flyers in small, high-technology companies. The shares of this fund lost 59.6 percent of their value during 1984. For every dollar you put into it in January, you would have ended the year with 40 cents.

Does this mean the Prudential-Bache people are smarter than the 44 Wall Street people? Is their planning sounder? Their thinking more astute? Not necessarily. It does mean that, in 1984, the managers of the Prudential-Bache Fund were luckier. In that year, for a thousand different reasons, the investment community as a whole felt optimistic about utility companies, so those companies' share prices rose. As a result, shareholders of the Prudential-Bache Fund ended the year with a nice Christmas present. But 1984 was a year of pessimism for the kinds of companies 44 Wall Street likes, so that fund's shareholders ended the year poorer than they wished.

Luck—that's all it was. There is no explanation that makes more sense. There is no reason to suppose the managers of the Prudential-Bache Fund are smarter as a group than those at 44 Wall Street. When mutual funds are hiring talent, they all scoop from the same pool. Every fund has on its staff some smart people and some dumb people. No fund will admit that it hires dumb people, but of course all organizations do. You can assume, therefore, that all large mutual funds are about equal in their general level of brightness and talent.

They differ in their approaches to investment; but no approach, viewed dispassionately, is measurably smarter than any other. The differences in their yearly results stem largely from one factor, one alone. In any given year, some are luckier than others.

NOW LET'S SEE what this knowledge does for you. How valuable is it to know that your fate in a given venture is going to be determined largely by luck?

The value is enormous.

We won't hang around Wall Street much longer, but let's take a last brief look at those mutual funds. Let's suppose you are the kind of person who ignores or denies the role of luck in money ventures. Some time in 1985 you chance to read about those 1984 mutual fund results. You note Prudential-Bache's gain of nearly 40 percent in its share value. "Wow!" you say. "These people are obviously smarter than the rest. They've got the stock market figured out!"

The state of having something figured out is presumed to be a permanent state. If it's figured out now, it will be figured out tomorrow. If Prudential-Bache was smart in 1984, the smartness will carry into future years. Or so you believe. You bet your wad on it. Bad luck enters the picture, and—*whomp!*—you end on your financial behind, wondering what happened.

Ignoring the role of luck is a recipe for bad luck. In fact, the tendency to make this mistake is one of the most notable characteristics of the chronically unlucky: life's losers.

But when you clearly see how luck affects a given situation, then you become strongly aware that the situation is bound to change. It can change radically, rapidly, without warning, in unpredictable ways. You cannot know what the change will be or when it will happen, but you can be perfectly sure it will happen sooner or later. The one thing you cannot expect is the very thing the loser *does* expect: continuity, a repetition of yesterday's events.

The loser's problem lies in the inability to make the crucial distinction between planning and luck. In the case of a mutual fund, it is *other people*'s planning we are talking about. In the case of Paula Wellman's roulette-playing friend, what tripped her up was a mistaken conclusion about her *own* planning.

Either way, the unlucky mental process is the same. The process begins when a good result occurs once or a few times. The loser studies it, ascribes it to planning, and concludes that the same planning will produce the same result in the future. And the loser loses again.

The lucky personality avoids getting trapped in that way. This isn't to say he or she avoids taking risks. Quite the contrary, as we will see later. What it does mean is that the lucky personality, entering a situation and perceiving it to be ruled or heavily influenced by luck, deliberately stays light-footed, ready to jump this way or that as events unfold.

The lucky approach is to say to yourself, "Okay I'm going to get into this risky situation—this roulette game, this mutual fund investment. But I am not operating under the delusion that planning will make it turn out my way. I see luck looming large in it, so I will be careful not to let myself grow too confident and relaxed. I will expect rapid change. I won't make large, irrevocable commitments. I'll stay poised to bail out the minute I see a change I don't like."

THERE ARE OF course many kinds of ventures in life that are not as heavily influenced by luck as are gambling and stock market investments. Planning may be more important than luck in much of what you do. The trick is to know what kind of situation you are in at any given time. Can you rely on your own or others' planning, or will the outcome be determined by luck?

To take a simple and familiar example: Driving a car is a situation in which you can generally rely on planning. You almost always get to your planned destination. True, bad luck can upset your plan. You might be hit by a drunk driver before you get where you're going. But the likelihood of such a random occurrence is not great. The situation is one in which planning clearly rules over luck, ninety-nine to one.

A somewhat more complex example is a sports event. I once watched the great Billie Jean King play tennis against an amateur in a charitable fund-raising event. In this case, the outcome was determined almost entirely by Ms. King's planning. She won the game because she *planned* to win. She had been perfecting her game ever since she started playing under professional coaching as a grade school girl. Only by the most unlikely stroke of luck could an amateur have beaten her. Thus, the influences on that game were just about the same as those on driving a car: 99 percent planning, 1 percent luck.

But a week later, Ms. King was back on the pro tournament circuit, struggling against players like Chris Evert Lloyd. Now the luck/planning ratio was more like fifty-fifty.

It is essential to arrive at some idea of this ratio in the important ventures of your life. Your career, your marriage if you're in one, your investments. Obviously, you won't be able to arrive at precise numbers: 57 percent planning, 43 percent luck. To attempt that would be silly. But you can develop a general awareness of luck's relative influence in your life's various situations. It may not be precise, but it is bound to be useful.

In studying the more complicated of your life situations—career and marriage, for example—you are likely to find that luck's influence is larger than you ever allowed yourself to believe. Finding this out can be a shock. But cheer up. The very act of finding it out can automatically improve your luck.

Consider the career adventures of Wendell R. Osborne, for instance. Osborne is an executive of a building-products company. His age is about fifty-five. Twice during his life—the first time in his late thirties, the second time in his forties—he found himself out on the street without a job. The first time, the experience devastated him; the second time, having become a student of luck, he was hardly troubled at all. Indeed, he was able to use the experience to his own advantage.

I met him at the Forty-Plus Club of New York, where he turned up during that second tour of joblessness. I had gone there specifically to collect some stories and wisdom about luck. The Forty-Plus clubs, which exist in major American and European cities, are in business for the sole purpose of helping middle-aged men and women find jobs. If you are over forty, have lost an executive-level job, and are having trouble finding a new one, you join a Forty-Plus Club. The club gives you general job-hunting help, special help in battling age discrimination, and—most important—a boost in morale. All the members are men and women between jobs. As soon as you land a job, you leave. It is an excellent place for hearing tales of good and bad luck.

Wendell Osborne told me his story. As a young man he joined the old Rath Packing Company, a big Iowa producer of processed meats. An older executive took a fatherly liking to young Osborne, helped him get some special training, maneuvered him into a production-line foreman's job, and then into a junior managerial position.

"I was good at what I did," he reminisced later, sitting comfortably in a sagging old armchair at the Forty-Plus Club. "I really was good at task management: making plans, foreseeing problems, motivating people to get the job done, all that. I was so good at it that I lost sight of the other strong forces in my life. I lost sight of luck."

Today he sees clearly that at least half the credit for his early success was due to luck. He would not have moved upward so fast—indeed, perhaps would not have moved upward at all—were it not for the older man who became his mentor. How did he happen to meet that older man, and how did their mentor-protégé relationship become established? Purely by luck: a chance meeting under the right circumstances in the parking lot. Young Osborne had helped the older man change a flat tire. Osborne's very presence in the parking lot at that particular time was itself a fluky circumstance, for he did not himself own a car and was walking across the lot "for no special reason; I was just ambling around."

At least half the credit for his career success, therefore, could be assigned to the trivial detail of a rambling walk—a chance turn in one direction instead of another. Thinking about his early career today, Osborne can identify other turning points at which luck played an influential role in the same way. But back then, he gave no credit to luck. He thought he was rising in the business world because of his managerial skills alone.

Like Paula Wellman's friend analyzing roulette outcomes and like a neophyte investor studying mutual fund performances, young Wendell Osborne thought of the major influences on his life as permanent. He had his managerial skills today; he would have them tomorrow. His tomorrows, therefore, were secure.

That was what he thought.

But the old Rath Packing Company ran into unforeseen economic changes that were eventually to cause its death. With shocking suddenness, a robust company started to come apart. There were plant closings, curtailments, mass layoffs. In the executive offices, frightened men and women fought and clawed for survival. Young Osborne's mentor was forced into early retirement, and a short time later, Osborne himself, no longer protected, was out on the sidewalk.

He was stunned. He did not know what had happened to him. He had had his life all planned. His security had seemed guaranteed. How could his Life Plan have fallen apart so abruptly? He still had the same skills today as yesterday, didn't he? Then how could it be—*how?*—that the security he had enjoyed yesterday was gone today?

These were the anguished questions that the unlucky young man asked himself. In time, he understood the answers—and never forgot them.

He found a new job in time—but only after going through a lot of personal pain and coming to the brink of personal bankruptcy. He resolved never to let himself become that vulnerable again. When he started his new job—with a medium-sized manufacturing company in

New Jersey—he kept his eyes wide open and observed the quiet workings of luck in his career.

As had happened at Rath, he moved upward fast. He *was* good at what he did, and when luck put him in the right places at the right times, he was able to take advantage of the situation. But he never repeated his previous mistake. He recognized his skills as valuable, but he did not delude himself into thinking that his rise was brought about by skill alone. "I'm where I am partly because of good luck," he kept reminding himself. "But luck can change. Luck is lifting me up today. *Tomorrow it may drop me.*"

With this reminder constantly in front of him, he prepared for the day when his luck might change in unknowable ways. The day might never come, but he acted always as though it would be tomorrow. Even when his career seemed to be going just right, even when he could have been feeling unassailably secure, he refused to let himself relax. He continually explored possibilities for other jobs. He questioned friends who worked for other companies. When an executive recruiter approached him with a feeler involving a job in Europe, he did not turn the man away with a "No, I'm happy where I am." Instead he went out of his way to befriend the recruiter, made a point of reestablishing contact with the man once or twice a year.

"I always knew exactly what I'd do if my job disappeared," he recalled. "I knew just what phone calls I'd make, what letters I'd write. I even looked into the Forty-Plus Club. Most people don't do that until *after* they've been kicked out in the street. I did it while I was still employed and feeling secure."

Finally, it happened to him again; he lost his job. He says little about the cause, except that it involved a costly error of judgment made by a senior executive. The blame sifted downward and landed on the shoulders of Wendell Osborne, now in his late forties.

It was the kind of bad luck that can hit anybody in a business organization. It was unpredictable. But in a way Osborne *had* predicted it. He had kept telling himself his luck could change.

And when it did change, he was ready. The normal length of stay in the

Forty-Plus Club is about three months. Wendell Osborne had three job offers within two weeks. The job he accepted came with a nearly 50% increase in salary.

WENDELL OSBORNE AND Paula Wellman's friend got into trouble by mistakenly thinking that certain good outcomes were brought about by good planning. The obverse also happens, though not as often: Knocked down by a bad outcome, the unlucky personality ascribes the loss to personal failings, ignoring the role of bad luck.

This is the "tragic flaw" theory, which we looked at briefly in an earlier chapter. For unknown reasons, literature teachers are in love with it. Nothing bad ever happens because of bad luck, according to this theory. Whatever went wrong for Hamlet or poor old Macbeth, supposedly, it was their own fault. Similarly, if you lose your job in a corporate upheaval, your spouse in a marital dispute, and your life savings in a stock market crash, the postulated reason is that you have some kind of tragic flaw.

Don't you buy it. That kind of thinking leads to unnecessary discouragement: "What's the matter with me?" In all likelihood nothing is the matter. You've just been hit by ill luck, that's all. Pick yourself up and try again.

The "tragic flaw" idea is good fun to toy with in a high school English class, but it has little relationship to real life. In real life, good and bad luck rule just as often as skills or flaws. When misfortune strikes, examine the event dispassionately. Maybe it *was* wholly or largely your fault. Maybe you did something dumb or lacked some skills that might have saved you. On the other hand, maybe the event was ruled 90 percent by luck. If so, don't be ashamed to say so.

Dr. Nancy Edwards, a New York psychotherapist, says it is characteristic of some of her most troubled patients to blame themselves for events that aren't really their fault. In many cases these are people who seem to have been dogged by bad luck all their lives: chronic losers. Dr. Edwards does not use that term, but it is clear she is describing a type of man or woman who would never make it in Atlantic City or on Wall Street.

For instance, one patient, a woman in her forties, had a long history of downward mobility in her career. She would work at a job for a year or two, get hit by some kind of bad luck, blame some failing in herself, and quit in a spasm of gloom and discouragement. Then, believing herself incapable of handling a job on that level of difficulty, she would seek a new job lower down the scale.

Her problem was, in one sense, the opposite of Wendell Osborne's. He failed to recognize the role of good luck in his early success, and Dr. Edwards's patient failed to recognize the role of bad luck in her job difficulties. But both were making the same fundamental mistake. Both looked exclusively inside themselves for explanations of what was happening to them. That is a recipe for bad luck.

The lucky personality looks outside as well as inside. Admittedly that isn't always easy to do, for it argues with some of our most cherished old Work Ethic preachments. We are told in school, in church, and in management-training seminars that we are the shapers of our own lives and the authors of our own outcomes.

But you should not believe it. It is nonsense. The first step in controlling your luck is to recognize that it exists.

# 4. The Second Technique: Finding the Fast Flow

When Lauren Bacall was young, she went out of her way to befriend a large number of people and get involved in a fast flow of events. So did Kirk Douglas. If they had not behaved in that way, we would not know either of their names today.

Talent? Of course they had talent. Also wit, charm, grace, and a lot of other good attributes. But none of it would have done either of them the least bit of good without luck. Their oddly linked stories illustrate with beautiful clarity how men and women find good luck by positioning themselves where events are flowing fastest.

Bacall, born Bacal, was a struggling young actress and model in New York during the early years of World War II. New York is always swarming with such hopefuls. Most are lovely and many are genuinely talented. They all seem to come from remote towns, where they reigned as beauty queens, led the Fourth of July parade and acted in the high school senior play. Now they are in the Big Apple, trying to get the world to pay attention.

Most are doomed to bitter disappointment. For of all those thousands of beautiful and talented young aspirants who pour into the great city each month, only a few can be chosen for national or even local prominence. Those with an obvious lack of talent will of course be rejected rapidly, but that still leaves thousands, tens of thousands. They all have talent, and since it cannot be measured, it must be assumed they have it in roughly equal amounts.

What determines success or failure for those young women? How are the few winners chosen? They are chosen by luck. The winners in this huge, eternal, and desperate lottery are those who chance to be in the right place at the right time.

Such was young Lauren Bacall's happy outcome. Her first couple of years in New York were attended by almost continuous bad luck, according to her autobiography, *By Myself.* She got bit parts in plays that promptly folded, landed modeling jobs that turned out badly for random reasons. Unconsciously practicing the First Technique, she recognized the bad luck for what it was. She saw correctly that the bad outcomes were in no way her fault, and therefore, she might as well go on struggling as long as her stamina lasted.

So she went ahead and applied the Second Technique. This, too, was unconscious on her part. There is no indication in her autobiography that she ever gave serious thought to the principles of luck control. She was simply one of those people who apply most of the principles without thinking about them—and who end up lucky without knowing why.

The commandment of the Second Technique is: *Go where events flow fastest.* Surround yourself with a churning mass of people and things happening.

Young Lauren Bacall did that without realizing that she was thereby increasing her chances of getting a lucky break, the break without which she could not go anywhere. She did not permit her string of bad luck to discourage her. Instead of becoming depressed and inactive—which bad luck can do to people when they believe it is caused by their own flaws—she kept herself oriented to the fast flow. She got busily, almost frantically involved in war-effort work such as the Stage Door Canteen; in part-time jobs such as ushering at theaters; in social events, dates, parties, and picnics. She made herself the center of a howling whirlwind of people.

She could not know which of those people would be the conduit through which her break would flow. As it turned out, that destiny-marked person was an obscure English writer named Timothy Brooke. He and Bacall weren't lovers. He was simply an affable man whose company the gregarious young would-be actress enjoyed. One night they went to a nightclub named Tony's. While there, Brooke introduced her to a casual acquaintance of his, a man named Nicolas de Gunzburg. She did not know it at the time, but this was the first link in a long chain of circumstances leading to her big break.

De Gunzburg was an editor of *Harper's Bazaar.* Through him, the lucky young actress got to know Diana Vreeland, the magazine's fashion editor. Vreeland gave her some modeling assignments. One arresting full-page shot caught the attention of a Hollywood producer, Howard Hawks. Lauren Bacall's movie career was launched.

She was a woman of great grace, beauty, and talent. Those attributes played a necessary part in her climb. She had to have them so that she could take advantage of the big break when it came. But she also had to have the break itself. If she had not gone out of her way to find the fast flow, and if she had not met that obscure British writer as a result, the name Lauren Bacall would mean nothing to us today.

LAUREN BACALL SEEMS not to have thought very profoundly about luck. Perhaps this was because she was naturally a lucky personality and, therefore, did not feel any great need to worry about it. She lived life as it came and found most of it enjoyable. But at the time when she was going through her early struggles in New York, hoping for her big break, she met a young man who did spend a good deal of time wondering about the role of luck in his own and others' lives. His name was Issur Danielovitch; and he came from Amsterdam, New York. He was trying to find work as an actor. His stage name was Kirk Douglas.

Many, many years after those tough times in New York, I interviewed Douglas in his agent's office in Hollywood. He recalled thinking consciously about fast-flow orientation, though he did not use that term. As an unknown young actor in New York, working at a Schrafft's restaurant to keep himself from starving, he realized clearly that the break he needed would come to him, if it came at all, through some other person. He could not know who that other person would be. But he *could* know that his chances of getting a break improved in direct proportion to the number of people he knew.

"If you're a hermit, nothing ever happens in your life," he said. "If you're the opposite of a hermit, things happen." He was the opposite of a hermit. In his time off from Schrafft's, he got himself involved in a whirl of people and events. One person he got to know was a young would-be actress named Lauren Bacall.

At the time, it seemed highly unlikely that this unknown young woman in the bargain basement clothes could ever be the conduit of special luck for him. She had no power or contacts in high places. If Kirk Douglas had engineered his social life with the cynical goal of meeting the rich and powerful, he would have ignored this Lauren Bacall. But so cynical and narrow-focused an approach isn't likely to produce good luck. The lucky personality gets to know everybody in sight: the rich and the poor, the famous and the humble, the sociable and even the friendless and the cranky.

We noted in the previous chapter that it is in the nature of luck to bring about fast, profound, unforeseen changes in situations—also in people. This is what happened to the hopeful young actress Kirk Douglas befriended. Her big break came and swept her off to Hollywood. In time, she was able to get some movie industry doors opened for him. Kirk Douglas followed her to stardom in the late 1940s.

Thus was her good luck translated into good luck for him. The whole long chain of circumstances was able to take place because both of them found the fast flow. If either one of them had failed to do that, neither Kirk Douglas's acting talent nor the arresting cleft in his chin would have done him any good. We would not know his name or face today.

WHETHER YOU ASPIRE to get into the movies or simply get a higher-paying or more exciting job, the rule is the same. Go where events flow fastest.

Eric Wachtel, a New York management consultant and executive recruiter, has watched literally hundreds of men and women climbing career ladders. In his observation, people who get dead-ended are very often people who allow themselves to become isolated.

"This doesn't mean you have to be one of those Personality Kids who know everybody in town," Wachtel says. "We can't all be the life of the party. Some of us are quieter than others. But we *can* all go around with a look and attitude that says we want to be friendly. We can stay active. The worst thing you can do is withdraw from the network of friendships and acquaintanceships at home and at work. If you aren't in the network, nobody is ever going to steer anything your way."

In the business world as in the movies, the big breaks flow through contacts between people. Not necessarily close friendships, just contacts—sometimes tenuous ones. The distant engine of fate begins to roll closer when, at the end of a long chain of distant events, A quits her job. It is offered to B, who is interested but who veers off in another direction when his old friend, C, offers him something better. D, an impartial observer of all this, has lunch one day with E and mentions the job opening. It sounds to E as though it might be something that would interest F.

E and F are not bosom buddies. They are casual acquaintances— occasional after-work drinking partners, perhaps, or fellow volunteers in some weekend Girl Scout activities. Neither would put the other on a list of "best friends." Still, E likes F, knows enough about her to guess what kinds of career openings would interest her, and is pleased to be the conduit of a potential break. When F hears about the distant job opening, she goes for it, gets it, and changes her life.

People are sure to be jealous of F. "That lucky so-and-so!" they will say. "Always in the right place at the right time!"

But *why* is she in the right places at the right times? Because she has made the effort to be in many places at many times. Fate has given her a lucky break, but she has earned it. She has *positioned* herself for it.

THE POWER OF seemingly weak links between people is one of the less well understood phenomena of human society. We know a lot about the strong links—more than we want to know, sometimes. Psychiatrists and psychologists eternally study sex, love, family ties, close friendships (and later in this book, we will study a special kind of friendship called destiny pairing). But what of the weak links? We don't pay much attention to them, though they may exert the most profound influence on our lives.

Think of all the people who know you on sight and by name, but whom you would not call "close." The neighbors you see a few times a year at parties. The woman who cuts your hair. The people down the hall at work. Your youngster's favorite teacher. The men and women who sing with you in the church choir or worked on last year's political campaign with you. The list goes on and on. If you are in the fast flow, you should be able to count a hundred of these weak-link contacts easily and another hundred or more after a little thought.

A social science team at the Massachusetts Institute of Technology once estimated that the average American is directly in contact with as many as five hundred people. This total includes strong as well as weak links, and it also includes extremely flimsy contacts—for example, your nodding acquaintanceship with some of the checkout cashiers at your local supermarket. These people recognize your face and enjoy chatting with you about the weather or food prices. You aren't a stranger, but that is about as far as it goes. They don't know your name or anything else about you, so it is hardly plausible to imagine that they might some day bring you a lucky break of any consequence. For purposes of our studies of luck, we won't include those very flimsy contacts in our definition of "weak links."

A better definition was developed once by a Harvard-funded psychologist, Dr. Stanley Milgram. He was interested in what psychologists call the "small-world phenomenon"—the often astonishing way in which people's networks of weak links overlap. You meet a total stranger on an airplane, strike up a conversation, and discover, to your amazement, that you both know the same person. "Yes, it's a small world!" you agree.

It certainly is, and Dr. Milgram determined to find out just how small. His studies are directly relevant to our studies of luck. When you have a clear appreciation of how very small this "small world" of ours really is, you will be in a better position to understand why getting into the fast flow can bring a startling improvement in luck.

In considering networks of person-to-person contacts, Dr. Milgram included both strong and weak links. But he excluded the very tenuous contacts such as a nodding acquaintanceship with a supermarket cashier. He was interested only in contacts in which there was "some meaningful, personal interaction"; and he defined those as contacts with people you know on a first-name basis. That is as good and quick a definition as any. Those are the "weak links" we are talking about: people you know on a first-name basis but would not classify as close friends or family.

Dr. Milgram picked a "target person" at random: a woman who lived in Cambridge, Massachusetts, and was married to a divinity student. Then he picked a small group of "starting persons" in Wichita, Kansas. Wichita was chosen at random, and so were the so-called starting persons. Each starting person got a letter from Dr. Milgram. It said, in effect:

> This is a study of the "small-world phenomenon." Enclosed is a document addressed to a lady living in Cambridge, Massachusetts. If you know this lady on a first-name basis, please see that it gets to her. If you don't know her, please pass it along to somebody whom you know on a first-name basis and who, in your judgment, *might* know her.

The object of this odd exercise was, of course, to see how long a chain of weak links would be needed to get back to the target person. Dr. Milgram asked people to guess how long the shortest chain would be. Most thought it would be one hundred links or more.

To Dr. Milgram's own astonishment, one chain completed itself in three links. A farmer in Wichita—one of the original "starting persons"—passed the document along to a minister friend. That man sent it to a minister he knew in Cambridge. The Cambridge minister knew the target woman, and the chain was finished.

Of the chains that were completed, the longest had ten links, and the median number was five. A startling result. Yet it becomes less startling when you look at the mathematics of it. Let's suppose you have first-name contacts—strong and weak links—with three hundred people. Let's further suppose that each of *them* has an average of three hundred links. This means that your secondary links—friend-of-a-friend—would total some ninety thousand people. And your tertiary links—friend-of-a-friend-of-a-friend—would total twenty-seven million.

With numbers like that, it is not surprising that the median chain in Dr. Milgram's experiment had only five links. By getting to know only three hundred people, you become a member of an enormous network of acquaintanceship.

But is it really that enormous? Are you really linked in a meaningful way with those twenty-seven million tertiary contacts?

Yes, indeed you are. Luck flows along linked chains of people until it hits targets, just as Dr. Milgram's document did. The flow very often begins with a friend-of-a-friend-of-a-friend.

Let's suppose you are bored, lonesome, stagnating and in need of a life-changing love affair to get your engine tuned up again. You have a weak link with a man named A, a fellow member of a local political action group. One night A's friend B, whom you don't know, gives a party. A, discovering that you are at loose ends that night, asks B if it's all right to bring you along. B says sure, as long as you contribute a bottle. Another guest is B's friend C, known to neither you nor A. This C, a tertiary link in your network, is the life-changing person you have been waiting for.

That is how luck happens.

As your great love affair with C grows and blossoms, some of your friends may be jealous. "What luck!" they will complain. "Why doesn't anything like that ever happen to *me?*" Perhaps because they are not in the fast flow. Your luck came to you because you knew A, along with 299 other people.

WE NOTED BEFORE that a mere nodding acquaintanceship—"Hi, how are you? Some weather, huh?"—is too weak a link to be thought of as a potential conduit for the flow of luck. It will be useful, to ask *in what way* it is too weak. Principally, in one way: The other person doesn't know enough about you.

The kinds of luck that this Second Technique is concerned with—the breaks that flow to a target person along linked chains of people—cannot easily reach a target who is only a face seen in a supermarket. To be singled out as a lucky target, you must make something of yourself known to those who are your primary links in the network. These can still be what we've called "weak" links, but they must be at least strong enough so that people know who you are, what work you do, what your interests are, what kinds of rewards you look for in life.

*It is necessary for them to know what you would consider a lucky break.*

An appealing fact about our sometimes unappealing species is that, with exceptions, we enjoy bringing each other lucky breaks. We like to be the bearers of good tidings. In the words of Eric Wachtel, the consultant recruiter: "It really is very pleasant to pick up the phone and say, 'Hey, Charlie, there's a job opening that sounds as if it might be your kind of thing.'" But before people can target you for that kind of benign treatment, they must know what it would take to make you happy.

As Wachtel puts it, "If I'm trying to fill a certain job, naturally I'll go to people I know about or people I can find out about. There may be a lot of other good candidates around, but if they keep themselves hidden, obviously, their phones are never going to ring." Your phone starts to ring when you feed the basic facts about yourself into the network.

It doesn't happen only in the world of jobs and careers. Donna Metzger, an Atlanta woman, tells a story of what she calls "amazing" luck in selling a pair of Colonial-era dolls. When you examine the story, it becomes less amazing. The luck flowed to Donna Metzger because she found the fast flow and made her wants known to people.

The two dolls in question had been in her family for many generations, handed down through a long progression of grandmothers and grand-daughters. By the time Donna received them, they were badly in need of repair and cleaning. She did not want to undertake that work herself, having no interest in doll collecting. On the other hand, she did not want

**47**

to throw the dolls away, for she recognized that they might have a good deal of value for a collector. They were genuine handmade antiques.

She wanted to give them away or sell them. The trouble was that she knew no doll collectors. The hobby is not a popular one like collecting coins or stamps. What could she do?

She wondered about placing ads in newspapers but postponed that decision. Meanwhile, she talked about her dilemma with people she knew. She knew many, being fast-flow oriented.

She had a weak link with a woman at a local tennis club. That woman talked frequently by phone with her brother—a strong link. During one phone conversation, the subject of antiques or collectors came up, and the woman mentioned the dolls that were perplexing her tennis-playing acquaintance, Donna Metzger. The brother said it was funny she should mention that, for he knew a woman who was an avid collector of antique dolls. The woman was a neighbor in the Philadelphia suburb where he lived. And so the chain was completed.

The doll-collecting woman, who thus acquired two rare items for a low price, undoubtedly felt she had been luck-blessed just as Donna Metzger did. Both women must have gone around telling the story in tones of awe: "I had the most amazing stroke of luck!" But was it really amazing? The two women were tertiary links in each other's networks of acquaintanceship. Both made the completion of the chain possible by making themselves and their wants known to a lot of people.

A very similar story is told by a Connecticut woman. In her case, however, the result of luck's flow was not merely to bring together a buyer and seller of a hobbyist's item. It was to bring together a father and daughter.

Her mother had died in childbirth. Her father, unable to take care of her, had given her up for adoption. She knew this much and a few other details of her parents' lives and her infancy. Since her teens she had been obsessed with the wish to be reunited with the father she had never known. Now she was in her forties and had just about given up hope of finding him. However, she was a naturally gregarious woman. She was

48

involved in a lot of activities, knew a lot of people, and talked often of her long hunt for her father.

The chain began to form in exactly the same way as with Donna Metzger's Colonial dolls. Somebody talked to somebody else and got the "funny you should mention that" reaction. As it turned out, there was a man living in California who often talked about a daughter he had last seen as a baby. The man's age and some other clues made a pattern that seemed to hang together. The chain was complete.

"What astounding luck!" everybody said. But was it?

GO WHERE EVENTS flow fastest. Specifically what does that mean? It means, simply, make contact with people. Get involved. Don't be a sideliner, watching events flow past. Plunge into the events yourself.

At work, counsels Eric Wachtel, go out of your way to make yourself known in your own company and outside it. Go to meetings, even boring ones. Join employee after-hours groups. Seek work assignments that will force you out beyond the little knot of people you usually associate with—your "home clump," as Wachtel calls it. And all the time, make your career goals known to those you meet.

In off-the-job life, be just as much of a meeter and joiner. As Wachtel says, it isn't necessary to try to be the local popularity king or queen. You can't fake vivacity. The tinny quality is quickly detected; the effort is tiring; and in any case, it isn't called for. If you're a quiet person, then be quiet. All that is necessary is that you meet a lot of people and let them know just who you are.

Group activities are ideal: glee clubs, political advocacy groups, whatever your interests may be. If you are wedded to a solitary pursuit such as stamp collecting, at least try to get involved in clubs and conventions devoted to the hobby. Also, go to parties. Give parties. Attend rallies. March in marches. If you exercise for fitness, don't exercise alone; join the Y.

Consistently lucky people are nearly always to be found in the fast flow. I never met one who was a recluse or even reclusive.

# 5. The Third Technique: Risk Spooning

There are two ways to be an almost sure loser in life. One is to take goofy risks; that is, risks that are out of proportion to the rewards being sought. And the other is to take no risks at all.

Lucky people characteristically avoid both extremes. They cultivate the technique of taking risks in carefully measured spoonfuls.

Some people find this an especially hard technique to come to grips with. In some cases they can appreciate its truth in an abstract way but find themselves incapable of putting it to practical use in their daily lives. Difficulties over this profoundly important Third Technique are among the most prominent causes of bad and mediocre luck. Study it with care.

OF THE TWO unprofitable extremes—goofy risks or no risks—by far the most commonly seen in our society is the latter. Large numbers of people in America and Western Europe shun risk as assiduously as they shun hornets. They value safety and security above everything. As a result, they miss some of life's best fun. And they tend to stay poor.

Consider the career plodder, a typical product of our place and time: joins a company right after high school or college; fears risk; never sticks her neck out; makes as few decisions as possible; innovates nothing. Comes to work promptly at opening time each morning, does precisely the work that is required, and goes home promptly at five. Thirty-five years later, collects a gold pen-and-pencil set and retires, never to be seen or heard from again.

What's it all for? Security. That is all the plodder has earned. A salary that bought modestly comfortable living conditions and a pension that assures a retirement free of want. Those are nice things to have, but where is the joy and color? Where are the great victories, the triumphs? They are missing.

Our education and social conditioning tend to push us into the plodder's way of life. We are taught that risk is foolish. The Puritan Ethic frowns on gambling and speculation. It urges us to make our way through life by keeping our noses to the grindstone: a bird in the hand and all that.

There is an old fable about a race between a tortoise and a hare. Schoolkids all over the world get this fable laid on them because it is supposed to teach a great truth about the proper way to design one's life. The prudent tortoise carefully conserves his capital—his energy—and wins. The crazy hare bets his entire capital in a single wild speculative spree, bankrupts himself early, and loses. The moral thus derived is that it is best to choose the plodder's way. That way may be boring, but it is the way to win. So says the ancient teaching.

But is it true? Not in real life, it isn't. The straight-line plodder, shunning risk, also avoids the possibility of lucky breaks. On the whole, plodders are unlucky.

Or perhaps it would be more accurate to say many of them are luck neutral. Neither good nor bad luck strikes them to any notable degree. Their lives hardly change. Nothing happens.

You may be reading this book partly because you feel you have been leading such a life. You don't necessarily have any grandiose dreams of becoming a movie star or making a six-figure killing on the stock market. You just want *something* to happen. You want interesting events. You want change.

But not even change will happen unless you take some kind of risk. Remember our definition of luck: events that influence your life but are not of your making. To secure the best chance that such events will happen to you, you have to *invite* them to happen; in other words, stick your neck out. You cannot control the kind of luck that will come your way. It may be good luck or bad. If it is bad, there are steps you can take to get out of its way. We will study those steps later in the book. For now, the point to understand is that if you want luck to come around and change your life, you must initially be willing to accept either good or bad luck. That is another way of saying *you must take a risk.*

YET OUR CULTURE keeps telling us not to take risks. It is a peculiar fact of life in America, and to a lesser extent in Western Europe, that some of the most solemn antirisk preaching comes from men and women whose early lives were in fact wildly risky. That odd phenomenon reinforces the basic Work Ethic philosophy of the culture and adds to the social pressures that turn too many people into risk-shunning plodders.

What happens is this: A man or woman (most often a man until recent times) indulges in some glorious speculation early in life. His luck is good. The speculation pays off. He becomes rich and famous. Young men and women look to him for advice. "How do *we* make it, sir?" all the new young climbers ask. And what does the revered sage reply? Does he tell the truth: that he made it by being lucky? Of course not. He says, instead, that he did it by being smart, dedicated, patient, tenacious, and all those Work Ethic things. He tries to make people believe that he is really just a pious plodder who happened to plod further than other people.

And strangely, most people believe him. Maybe that is because he gives them what seem like sound reasons for avoiding risk. A risk-free life seems safe and comfortable, and that is what most people choose when they see no good reason to choose otherwise.

John D. Rockefeller the elder was an early example of this phenomenon. In fact he was so good an example that he was very nearly a caricature of it.

Old John D. made his enormous pile by taking some wild gambles in the oil business. He began adult life as a half-starved young clerk in a Cleveland mercantile business. He recognized instantly that he was always going to be a half-starved clerk if safety was the guiding principle of his life. To lift himself above the lower or lower middle income strata, he realized he would have to take risks. And that is what he did. By saving and borrowing, he put little wads of capital together and plunged into various commodity speculations and other ventures. He had some bad luck but also some good. One excellent piece of luck (the result of Rockefeller's fast-flow orientation) was his meeting with a man named Samuel Andrews, an expert in the chancy new business of refining oil. Rockefeller by now was a practiced and dedicated risk taker, and the idea of a new gamble was a powerful attraction. He and Andrews set up an oil refinery in Cleveland, against a chorus of jeers from more sober businessmen who were sure it was a harebrained gamble. That Cleveland refinery was the nucleus of Standard Oil.

He was a risk taker of the first magnitude. No plodder, this Rockefeller was a man who stuck his neck out and invited luck to come and change his life.

But after he had made his first few hundred millions, and after he had become a nationally known source of Great Wisdom on how to succeed in life, did he ever mention luck? Did he counsel people to take risks? No. He told them to be plodders.

He became famous for singling out small, ragged boys—caddies on golf courses, newsboys on street corners—and delivering homilies on hard work, thrift, and patience. "Work hard, spend wisely, invest safely, and let time do the rest," he would solemnly instruct, as the wide-eyed kid gaped up at him. And then Rockefeller would reach into his pocket, pull out a dime, and plunk it into the youngster's small, grimy palm. "Save a dime every day," the tycoon would declare, "and you'll be a rich man!"

This was perfect nonsense, of course. Assuming the kid had seventy more years to live, his total invested capital after a lifetime of following Rockefeller's advice would be $2,555. If the kid was lucky, compounding interest at fluctuating rates might triple or quadruple the amount—to $10,000, let's say. Rich? Rockefeller himself earned that much money in a single day.

In any case, the whole dime-giving charade was a hoked-up public relations scheme. It was invented by Ivy Ledbetter Lee, Rockefeller's public relations counselor. The object of the game was to change old John D.'s image as a fast-buck operator and thereby ameliorate a storm of public criticism over certain Standard Oil business practices. Lee saw to it that the much-abused, often hated tycoon was always supplied with a pocketful of dimes. The old gentleman's valet was instructed, in fact, to consider the dimes as important as any item of clothing. The aged tycoon was no more to be allowed out of the house without his dimes than without his trousers. He was to seek out small boys in any place where news reporters were present, hand out dimes, and mumble about Work Ethic stuff. He was to hide, with the utmost care, the real truth about his stunning success: that he was a risk taker who got lucky.

And people swallowed it. Including, perhaps, some of those small boys who received dimes and advice. They would now be elderly men. Those who took the advice have plodded their way through life and can now boast small savings accounts, maybe. Few are rich. Few have climbed peaks of fun or triumph. Was it good advice?

WE HAVE NOTED before that it diminishes us to admit that our greatest achievements resulted largely or even partly from good luck. It is much more ego warming to say, "I made it because I was smart"—or because I had patience, fortitude, and all that. Undoubtedly this fear of diminishment was one reason why old John D. Rockefeller avoided talking about risk and luck.

But the more important reason—at least from the viewpoint of Ivy Lee, the public relations choreographer—was that there is something very un-Puritan about gambling. At the time that Rockefeller was assailing small boys with his dimes and advice—the early decades of this century—Standard Oil was embroiled in shrill arguments about corporate morality. The company was the target of muckrakers who accused it of illegal price-fixing, monopoly in restraint of trade, bribery of public officials, and other unsavory practices. Many of the charges were without foundation in fact, and many others, while plausible, were based on fairly flimsy evidence.

But the public believed many of the accusations because it *wanted* to. It wanted to because it hated Standard Oil, and it hated Standard Oil at least in part because the huge company's founder and figurehead, John D., had grown rich by luck. He had gambled and won. And in America, that can be a mistake.

Many people, especially of the plodder breed, hate a successful gambler. They hate him largely because they hate themselves for not having had the guts to take their own risks. He stands there rich, happy, and having a world of fun; a living advertisement for what they might have been. Seeking acceptable reasons to dislike him, they cultivate the notion that gambling is, in some way, impure.

That was one of the things that made Standard Oil so easy a target for muckrakers. Its founder and chief was a gambling man, obviously a fellow of low character and not to be trusted. Ivy Lee, perceiving this, invented the dime-giving game as one way of proving that old John D. *wasn't* a gambler. Why, no! He was just an ordinary nose-to-the-grindstone type like your next-door neighbor!

Thus, the antirisk mentality keeps its dominance. Even the very biggest risk takers and the very luckiest gamblers are determined to show they are nothing of the kind.

FOR A MORE modern example, consider Thomas John Watson, the man who founded mighty IBM. This tall, lean, ascetic, somewhat dour fellow made himself into perhaps the world's leading evangelist of the Work Ethic. He didn't look, act, or speak as though he had ever taken a risk in his life. Luck? The word never entered his conversation. He wouldn't allow anything so untidy as luck to play a part in projects *he* was associated with.

"Plan your work and work your plan," he told the crisp young men and women who came to work for him and emulated him. *That* was the route to success. Luck had nothing to do with it.

Watson's most famous slogan was "Think." Signs bearing that single word, in dozens of languages, hang in offices and factories all over the world. The slogan once was longer and even more stern. In the company archives, photographs of long-ago sales meetings show banners urging the assembled strivers to "Work and Think." Watson personally leaned toward a three-item slogan. Once when I, a young *Business Week* reporter, interviewed him and asked him the usual question about the roots of success, he wagged a bony finger at me and intoned solemnly, "Work, Think, and Plan."

It also helped, in his view, to have a starchy white shirt and well-shined shoes. I recall doing a lot of wriggling during that interview, trying to place my scuffed loafers where he couldn't see them.

Work, think, and plan. A man who could invent a slogan like that would have to be a dedicated champion of the Work Ethic. As far as I know, no more dedicated champion ever strode the earth than Thomas John Watson.

And yet Watson had risen to his high station by being a gambler. This man who claimed you could plan your way through life, this man who never mentioned luck, had in fact taken some wild risks in his younger days. His luck had held; he had won. But like John D. Rockefeller before him, he carefully ignored the workings of luck when young reporters came around to sample his wisdom.

His first encounter with luck was discouraging. He sold sewing machines door-to-door, raised some cash, and opened a food store in Buffalo, New York. Mainly because a bigger, better-funded rival store chanced to open nearby at the same time, Watson's venture failed quickly. It must have occurred to him that no amount of Working, Thinking, or Planning could have prevented this dismal outcome. At an early age—he was in his early twenties—he had been given an introduction to the mysteries of luck.

Next, he went to work as a salesman for the National Cash Register Company. After a chancy start, he worked his way into a secure job. Lifetime safety could have been his if he had wanted it, but he didn't. He chose, instead, to stick his neck out—far out.

It was a mad gamble. Three small office-machine manufacturers had merged into a clumsily glued-together outfit called the Computing-Tabulating-Recording Company. It had lost money from the start. Two presidents had tried to nurse it to health without success. Its aggregate bonded debt totaled three times its assets. Most of the major stockholders and directors wanted to bail out with a few cents on their dollars, but they couldn't find anybody dumb enough to buy their shares. Desperate, they hunted for a new president, somebody who knew something about office machines. The new man would have to be a gambler.

The gambler they found—a tertiary link in somebody's acquaintance-ship network—was Tom Watson. He was then about forty years old. He was looking for a change in luck and was willing to take an enormous risk for that purpose. Like Rockefeller in the previous century, he had come to understand that you cannot get rich on a salary. If he wanted to make a meaningful change in his life, he would have to embark on a gamble.

So he went to work for the half-dead company, CTR. He agreed that his salary should be only partly in cash. The other part was to be in the company's nearly worthless shares.

He had put himself at the mercy of luck. Of course he could work, think, and plan all day long, but the company's fate was only to a limited degree under his control. Luck was in the driver's seat, as it is with any weak company. CTR could have been killed by any of a thousand possible events not of Watson's making: economic changes, the appearance of a powerful competitor, and so on. By good luck, no such event happened. CTR survived, then prospered, and finally changed its name to IBM.

Back in 1914, when this risk taker first came to CTR, you could buy one hundred of the company's common shares for less than $3,000. By the time of Watson's death in 1956, stock dividends and splits had multiplied that round lot to 4,987 shares, and they were worth about $2,275,000.

And this was a man who never talked about luck.

J. PAUL GETTY knew. The old gentleman wrote thirty-four articles for *Playboy,* telling the readers how to make it financially in a hostile world where half one's friends and relatives were going broke. Listen to old Uncle Paul, Getty would say. You want to get ahead, young fellow? Then do as I have done. And he would list all the Work Ethic virtues that he believed had contributed to his stunning wealth. Have faith in yourself, he preached. Persevere. Practice thrift. Think clean thoughts. Quit smoking. (Getty was proud of that.) Study hard. Laugh at life's storms. You know: all that.

*Playboy* printed this stuff partly because of Getty's famous name and partly because he owned a piece of the company. A third reason—the man deserves his due—was that he wrote with considerable grace and verve. At one time in his youth he had wanted to be a writer. He was probably the world's most literate oil tycoon.

But all that stuff about getting rich by hard work, thrift, and fortitude was nonsense, and deep down in his heart, Jean Paul Getty knew it. "It was really luck, wasn't it?" I challenged him one day in a mischievous mood. He replied in mock alarm, "You've found me out!" Then he said, soberly, "Well, maybe. Luck. But who ever admits it was luck? How can you make a sermon out of luck?"

You cannot make a sermon out of luck. But if you want to know how Getty really founded his monumental fortune, the fact is that he and his heirs owe everything to luck in its purest, blindest, wildest form.

Getty made it by striking oil. His very first test well—mark that: *his very first*—was a 720-barrel-a-day gusher.

Virtue had nothing to do with it. Getty was not even looking for oil very seriously at the time. He had no plan to make oil his life's work. He was just larking around. In college, after toying with the idea of a literary career, he had become attracted instead to the diplomatic service. This new career plan pleased his father, a Minneapolis lawyer who had made some killings in Oklahoma oil. Young Jean Paul thereupon got himself sent to Oxford for polishing. He came back to America with a faint British accent and started looking into the diplomatic job market. But he was distracted by the fun being had in Oklahoma. He decided to delay the start of his government career and taste some of that fun for himself. With a modest stake from his father, he went into business—just for a year or so, he thought—as an oil wildcatter.

He spudded his first test well near the tiny Oklahoma town of Stone Bluff. The reasons for hoping there might be a flow of oil beneath that remote spot were no better than the reasons indicating a million other spots. But, early in February 1916, that out-of-the-way hole in the ground began spewing wealth into the startled young man's bank account.

That was the beginning of it all. He and his father founded the Getty Oil Company in May 1916, and young Jean Paul went on to become one of the richest men in the history of the world.

Why him?

Thrift? Courage? Diligence?

We know better. It was luck.

IT IS ESSENTIAL to take risks. Examine the life of any lucky man or woman, and you are all but certain to find that he or she was willing, at some point, to take a risk. Without that willingness, hardly anything interesting is likely to happen to you.

For a simple and commonplace example, consider state lotteries. As everybody knows, and as the lotteries' ads keep reminding us, you cannot win a prize unless you place a bet.

It isn't much money. A dollar or two will get you into the game in any state that runs a lottery. Yet even that small degree of risk seems to be too much for many people. Failing to get into the game, they are doomed to sit on the sidelines, watching jealously as more willing risk takers collect those stunning prizes.

One lucky risker was Lula Aaron, a New York grandmother. It was her habit for many years to buy a few state lottery tickets after finishing her Saturday grocery shopping. She would stop in at a liquor store near her favorite supermarket and risk a dollar or five dollars or something in between, depending on how she felt.

Some of her friends and neighbors felt this was a silly practice. The odds against winning were big, they pointed out. Buying those lottery tickets was like pouring money down the drain.

The fifty-four-year-old grandmother responded with a risk taker's credo. "I used to tell them I placed those bets because I *enjoyed* it," she explained to a lottery official. "Even if I never won, I got my dollar's worth of fun out of it every week. The fun was knowing I'd bought myself a chance to win." Or to put it another way, the act of taking this minor Saturday risk put her *in position* to win.

The people who criticized her were locked out of that position by their own choice. She had a chance to win, but they were bound to be losers.

Eventually she did win: $10 million, or twenty-one annual payments of $476,000. All taxable, of course, but who cared? Mrs. Aaron, the Saturday risker, was rich.

Undoubtedly many of those who criticized her were jealous. "Some people have all the luck!" they may have complained. But if they reflected on the episode, it should have occurred to them that their failure to win was their own fault.

NOT EVERYBODY IS interested in lotteries, of course. But the need to take risks extends into all areas of life. Falling in love, for instance. If you want to experience the joys of such a relationship, you must be willing to take the possible hurts, too. You must be willing to make an emotional commitment that has the capacity to wound you. But it is exactly like playing a lottery: If you don't bet, you are not in position to win.

Dr. John Kenneth Woodham, a New Jersey psychologist, observes that the unwillingness to take risks is a characteristic of those unlucky people we call "born losers." He says, "Not all losers have this risk-aversion thing, but I do see it often in the really beaten-down kind of person, the kind life has kicked in the teeth over and over again."

He tells of a patient whom he last saw about a year ago. He calls her Louise but says that is not her real name. "The minute she walked into my office, I could guess what her problem was or, at least, part of it: She was scared to make a move. She walked and sat in a head-down kind of way, avoided eye contact, even avoided talking about herself for the first couple of sessions. I mean she talked but not about what counted. She talked *around* things. She was afraid to take risks even with a therapist. She stayed closed up inside herself and stayed safe."

Louise's story came out slowly. "One dominant theme in her life," Dr.

Woodham recalls, "was an intense love-hate-rivalry kind of relationship with a former college roommate. Louise was in her middle thirties when I was seeing her, but this painful thing with the roommate seemed to be as strong as it had ever been when they were younger. All through the years, Louise kept comparing herself with this roommate—and in these comparisons, Louise always finished last. The roommate lived the kind of life Louise wanted: you know, glamorous, colorful, varied, and interesting. She had all the good successes, the great jobs, the grand passions with men. Louise envied her, hated her, then hated herself for being envious."

Louise's life was gray and dull by comparison. She lived with her mother in a suburban town. Years ago her roommate had suggested that they share an apartment in Boston, but Louise had found that too risky a proposition. Louise had a boring but secure job with an insurance company near her suburban home. She did not want to leave that corporate womb and look for a new job in Boston. What if nobody wanted to hire her? How would she pay the rent on that apartment? She would have to borrow. But then, suppose it took her a year or more to find a job with a big enough salary. What would she do then? How would she ever get out of debt?

She was so acutely worried about losing that she was unable to place a bet. Later, when the roommate was about to start a small business of her own and invited Louise to join her, Louise was again unwilling to take the risk.

The same problem stifled her relationships with men. Since it is never possible to be 100 percent sure about another person we have just met, every new relationship requires us to take a chance—sometimes a big one, sometimes a small one. Louise was never willing to place even a small bet. Dr. Woodham is not perfectly certain about this, but he suspects men found her unnecessarily suspicious, tense, and unresponsive—not the kind of woman with whom the average man would want to spend his Saturday nights.

Louise's roommate didn't win all her bets, any more than Lula Aaron, the lottery player, won all hers. But the roommate did place herself in position to win, and that positioning paid off. She ended up as the owner of a successful business, modestly wealthy, free to travel at will, married to a man she loved. Louise ended trapped in a life of loneliness and boredom.

ONE OF LOUISE'S difficulties evidently was that she lacked skill in assessing the risk-reward ratio in her life's important situations. Either that, or she didn't understand the need to make such an assessment. All risks looked equally daunting to her.

That is a recipe for poor positioning in the world of luck. It is essential to study risk-reward ratios. When a given risk is small and a potential reward large, you might as well take the risk and so position yourself to become a winner.

A risk may be "small" either in terms of its size or in terms of the odds against you. A simple example of a small-sized risk is a bet in a state lottery. You plunk down a dollar. The odds against you are huge. In all likelihood, you are going to lose that dollar. But since it is so small an amount, and since the potential six- or seven-figure prize is so big, you can justify taking the risk. As Lula Aaron noted, you can justify it on the basis of fun alone.

For an example of a risk that is "small" in terms of odds, consider the act of putting your money in a savings bank. The looked-for reward is the interest you expect the bank to pay you, and the risk is that the bank will fail with your money trapped inside it. If it fails, the Federal Deposit Insurance Corporation is supposed to reimburse you. It may do so, but only after a long delay and with no interest. If a lot of banks fail all at once in some world economic collapse, then there will be a "run" on FDIC, and it, too, will fail. In such a catastrophe, you probably will lose every dime of your deposit.

But the risk of that unhappy outcome is very small. This situation is exactly the opposite of the lottery bet. The reward you are seeking—the bank interest—is small. But the odds against you are also small. Thus, even though we may be talking about a big amount of money—your life savings—you can still consider the risk to be "small" and so can justify it.

Not all situations are so clear-cut, of course. Indeed, few situations are.

Life is a muddle of fogbound choices. One trait of the consistently lucky is that they are able to assess risk-reward ratios even amid this confusion and ambiguity.

Somebody like Louise, lacking this skill, may well come to see all risks as pretty much alike. If a possible course of action involves *any* degree of risk, then it is to be avoided.

A risk avoider like Louise will therefore shun gambles in which the risk is really quite small. For example, there was Louise's refusal to leave a secure job and go job hunting in Boston. In this case the potential reward was big, a grand package of assorted goodies: a better job, more money, more excitement, new kinds of fun in the city environment, and so on. Risk was involved, and that risk frightened Louise off.

But what was the risk? It was really not so big. The worst likely outcome was that she would be jobless for a few months. She would then have had to use up savings and perhaps borrow for living expenses. Not a calamity, just an inconvenience. She would not disappear off the face of the earth. There are no debtors' prisons in America. She would not be allowed to starve while down on her luck. Moreover, there were fairly good odds that this down period, if it happened at all, would last only a few weeks. As an able young woman with good job skills to offer, she was not likely to wait long before an employer took her off the market.

It was a gamble worth taking. It might have led to a big win.

AND THEN THERE are people who make the opposite mistake: taking big risks for small gains. They are very much more colorful people than the Louise type, and as a result we hear more about them. The dull gray life of a Louise isn't newsworthy, and its only contribution to fiction is to inspire a lot of boring novels and short stories in which nothing happens. But let some wild risk taker walk between skyscrapers on a tightwire, and that's news. It can be gripping fiction, too. Some of the world's best plays, novels, and movies are based on mad risks at Monte Carlo; on Wall Street; in war, poker, and love.

But in real life, those exciting and colorful people are not nearly as common as the risk avoiders. There are at least ten men and women of the Louise type for every reckless gambler.

The reckless ones are also far less well understood, which may help explain why we find them fascinating. You don't have to be a shrink to guess at the motives of a risk avoider. The risk-shunning syndrome stems from excessive fear of getting hurt, often as the result of being burned in the past or seeing a loved one burned. It's usually that simple. But what makes somebody into a compulsive gambler, betting the rent money on long shots? What strange fire rages in a woman who climbs dangerous mountains simply for the reward of standing at the top?

Nobody knows. There are a lot of psychoanalysts and others who say they know, but they don't. All that can be said for sure is that some people crave risk the way others crave alcohol or drugs. These risk cravers usually lose just as Louise did, only more spectacularly.

Such a man was Joe Kennedy, Jr., older brother of President John F. Kennedy. Joe was a compulsive risker. He was always involved in harebrained stunts—for instance, swimming across an icy, turbulent river that could easily have drowned him, just for the reward of saying he had done it. He lost a bundle speculating in the stock market, risking big amounts on ventures with appallingly long odds. His luck was almost certain to run out sooner or later, and it did. At the age of 29, during the Second World War, he volunteered to fly a near-suicidal bombing mission against a German rocket installation. He told a friend that the chances of success were only fifty-fifty. He never returned from the mission.

What draws people to such fearsome risks? Psychoanalysts speculate about a "death wish," but the existence of so weird a motivation has not been convincingly demonstrated. It probably doesn't exist except in a very few, very peculiar individuals. It certainly isn't a common trait among humans. Nor is the minor death wish that analysts ascribe to compulsive gamblers—the supposed wish to lose. In Freudian theory, a gambler may want to lose because he wants to be punished for some real or imagined sin or failing, usually a fantasized, sex-oriented sin supposedly committed in childhood.

Well, maybe it's so. I hope I may be forgiven for doubting it. In all my years of studying luck, in all my travels up and down Wall Street and around the casinos, I have never met a gambler of either sex who wanted to lose. Never. I very much doubt that there is such a person.

On the contrary, all gamblers want to win—including the pathological risk cravers who are always betting too heavily against the odds and losing. *All* of them want to win. The more compulsive ones—the daily long-odds bettors and chronic losers—are known to go crazy with delight when they do happen to win. They dance and sing, hug strangers, and walk into bars and buy drinks for the house. That isn't the behavior of somebody who secretly wanted to lose.

What really seems to drive such a risk craver is not a desire to lose but just the opposite: a desperate yearning for the experience of a big win. It must be a *big* win: a twenty-to-one shot at the track, a stock market gamble that pays off in six figures. Modest successes aren't enough for the risk craver. He is like a heroin addict who started by injecting small amounts of the drug, got hooked, built up a tolerance, and now, cannot get a kick except from large amounts.

Studies at Johns Hopkins University bear out this conclusion. At the university's Compulsive Gambling Counseling Center, staff members say they have never noticed any widespread "wish to lose" among their patients. Nor have they identified any special personality type as particularly prone to this problem. But according to project administrator Sandra Leavey, there are "common threads" in the lives of many of the patients.

Two of these common threads are worth looking at. First, the risk craver often turns out to have had a childhood in which gambling was accepted as a positive experience. The youngster went to the racetrack with Dad or heard a favorite aunt talk about the fun to be had in Las Vegas. And second, the risk craver had a big win early in his or her gambling or speculating career.

Thus, perhaps, an exaggerated urge to gamble becomes established. First, the future overrisker learns from an admired aunt that gambling is a good activity to be involved in. This is the opposite of the Puritan disapproval and bird-in-the-hand preachments most of us get as kids, and it sets the stage by *allowing* the neophyte risker to enjoy a jackpot without having feelings of guilt or uncertainty. Then, when a big win happens, the young risker gets a million-volt jolt of pure gambler's pleasure and is hooked for life.

ANYBODY WHO IS so thoroughly hooked into overrisking is probably not going to be changed by reading a book or listening to a lecture. Compulsive gamblers and speculators *know* their behavior is self-destructive without needing to be told so. All they need do is look at their own bank accounts to observe that they aren't lucky. As a general rule, somebody so hooked needs the special help provided by organizations such as Gamblers Anonymous. The members of GA, thoroughly and personally familiar with the risk craver's problems, are best equipped to help each other.

But statistically, if you feel good luck has been avoiding you, it is far more likely that you lean in the direction of too little risk taking rather than too much. What you must do is learn the technique of risk spooning.

From now on, seek out risks. Start small. The very least degree of risk you should expose yourself to is the degree associated with a typical state lottery, in which tiny amounts are bet against long odds in the hope of monumental rewards. If your state runs a lottery, bet a couple of bucks once in a while. Or place a bet when you visit a neighboring state.

If there's an office or neighborhood Super Bowl pool, get into it. Play bingo at the local church once in a while. Risk a few quarters in a slot machine if you get the chance. Buy raffle tickets. The idea is to get used to the idea of taking risks and to become comfortable with the thought of yourself as a prudent risker.

Take a few risks in your personal life. Get out of the habit—Louise's habit, and a very common one—of automatically shying away from every risk. Instead, assess the risk and determine if it is really as big as you supposed. If it is, and if the hoped-for reward is small, then all right, don't take the risk. But if it is minor and the potential reward is big, grit your teeth and place your bet.

This kind of risk assessment can become important in all kinds of situations. Potentially grand love affairs, friendships, and business relationships usually start with the need to take a chance on another person. New career opportunities almost always involve taking a chance. If you insist on waiting for risk-free situations, you are probably doomed to wait, like Louise. And wait. And wait.

Once you get used to risk, think about increasing the dosage. Don't keep all your money in a bank. Take a flier in the stock market. Invest in a friend's promising new business. You don't have to gamble with your entire net wealth; that would create an unacceptably high risk-reward ratio, the kind that has such a fatal attraction for GA members. But you must conquer your fear of risk.

No matter how you define success, risk is a necessary ingredient of every successful life. Risk puts you in position to win.

# 6. The Fourth Technique: Run Cutting

"Don't push your luck," says the ancient maxim. Only the lucky really understand what it means.

The unlucky are often taught its lesson by violent means, but the lesson seldom seems to stick. It is characteristic of the unlucky that they go on violating this adage again and again.

For instance, there was the unlucky couple who almost made a small fortune on Wall Street a few years ago. Their story was told to me by a Merrill Lynch account executive. Like many or most stories about inept handling of this Fourth Technique, it is a story that can make you want to cry.

This couple, a man and woman in their forties, had been in the stock market a long time, with discouraging results. Years back, she had inherited about $100,000 from her father. She and her husband decided to put it into the market in hopes of making it grow. In observance of the Third Technique, they were ready to take a risk. Too bad they didn't know about all the other techniques, too. They ran their $100,000 down to about $50,000.

Then, in the late 1970s, the beginnings of a lucky break loomed up. The couple lived and worked on the fringes of the television business, and one day, inadvertently eavesdropping, the woman overheard a hushed and tense conversation between two network executives. The conversation had to do with a man named Chuck Barris, producer of several well-known, zany quiz and talent shows such as "The Dating Game" and "The Gong Show." Barris's small company, Chuck Barris Productions, had been publicly held since the early 1970s. Its common shares were traded over-the-counter, but not very enthusiastically. In the five years preceding 1978, they had never risen any higher than 87.5 cents a share, and most of the time you could pick them up for 25 cents or so—if you wanted them.

The gist of the overheard conversation, however, was that exciting changes were afoot at Chuck Barris Productions. The changes were known so far only to a small, close-mouthed group of people. Soon the word was bound to spread to the show-biz community at large, and then, conceivably, the stock's market price could soar.

The woman rushed home to tell her husband the news. For several days they checked it out discreetly. It seemed to be a true scoop. The gossip was that Barris's little company was enjoying unusual prosperity and had some ambitious expansion plans.

The couple called their broker. He fed the stock's trading symbol, BCHK, into his desktop computer terminal and was astonished to learn that the bid price had more than doubled in the past month. It was now quoted at two dollars. The couple grew wildly excited. Their broker gave them the usual warning against buying stock on a hot tip, but they felt they had exercised proper prudence by checking the story with care before calling the broker. They believed a genuine, once-in-a-lifetime lucky break had fallen into their hands from heaven.

Over a span of a few weeks, they put some twenty-five thousand dollars into BCHK. This was about half the total worth of their brokerage account. It seemed like a large amount to bet. Indeed, it came perilously close to a compulsive gambler's style of overrisking. But they had been in the market so long without a payoff that they felt compelled to go after a big win.

As it turned out, BCHK was an even better buy than they had dared hope. By sheer good luck, they had stumbled into one of those rare situations in which, for a brief shining hour, everything a company touches turns to gold. Chuck Barris Productions seemed unable to make a mistake. All its gambles worked. Even dumb projects paid off. Money poured in.

And the stock price soared. After buying it at slightly more than two dollars a share, the happy couple watched popeyed as it jumped to nine dollars in less than a year. They had quadrupled their money in a space of a few months.

"Sell!" their broker urged.

He was right. They should have sold. They were enjoying a run of luck. As nearly all lucky people realize instinctively or learn through experience, runs of luck always end sooner than you wish. Sometimes they are long runs; much more often they are short. Since you can never tell in advance when a given run is going to end, the only sensible thing to do is preserve your gains by jumping off early in the game. *Always* assume the run is going to be short. *Never* try to ride a run to its very peak. *Don't push your luck.*

The couple could not make themselves sell out, however. They were gripped by greed. "If this stock quadrupled once," they said, "it could quadruple again, right?"

Right. It *could.* But the chances were against that. It is always a mistake to bet on a long run. As a matter of fact, most lucky people would have sold that stock long before it reached nine dollars a share. Having bought it at two dollars, many would have sold at four dollars. I would certainly have sold by the time it hit six dollars. To double or triple one's money in a few months is enough to ask of one's luck. Though it turned out later that the price would rise to nine dollars, it would have been irrational to *expect* that outcome or even to hope for it. The rational approach would have been to assume that you were in on a short run and that the ride was probably over at four dollars or six dollars.

The greed-gripped couple held on to their stock. Within a year it plummeted back to four dollars. They kept hanging on, hoping the company's fortunes would improve again. They didn't. Eventually the couple sold at seventy-five cents. They were losers again.

ALWAYS ASSUME A given run will be short. You will virtually always be right. The law of averages is heavily on your side.

The simplest way to illustrate this is to calculate the mathematics of probability in tossing a coin. If you toss it 1,024 times, the odds are there will be one long run in which heads comes up nine times in a row. But there will be thirty-two short runs in which heads comes up four times in a row.

Which is the way to bet? On the short runs, of course.

Let's say you have some money riding on this tossed coin. You are betting on heads. A run has started. Heads has come up four times in a row, and you have accumulated some winnings. What do you do?

Do you hope you are in on the beginning of a long run, maybe a run of nine heads in a row? And do you therefore let your money ride, praying for a big win? That would be the thinking process of the typical loser.

Or do you assume this run will be short, as most runs are? And do you therefore take your money out of the betting and put it in your pocket? That is the reaction of the lucky.

Always cut runs short. Sure, there will be times when you regret doing this. A run will continue without you, and you will be left enviously watching all the happy players who stayed aboard. But statistically, such gloomy outcomes are not likely to happen often.

Much more often, you will be thankful you left early. People will be puzzled when you quit, will call you foolish, and will try to urge you aboard again. "This run isn't about to end yet!" they will say. "Look at all the fun you're missing!" And then the boat will sink.

A peculiar characteristic of the genuinely lucky—at least it seems peculiar until you analyze it—is that they so often appear pessimistic. But it isn't pessimism; it is only run cutting. It is a rational approach to a world of unpredictable, uncontrollable events.

ONE PROBLEM IS that long, high runs of luck make news and get talked about. If you go to a racetrack and have a so-so day, you will forget it quickly. But if you have one of those days when every horse runs for your benefit, you will undoubtedly bore your friends with the story for a long time. We hear more about big wins than about the vastly more common little wins. This can delude us into thinking the big wins are more attainable than they really are. We think: "Well, if all these stories are true, maybe there's a big win waiting out there for *me.*"

So we push our luck, ride our runs too long—and sink.

Gambling casinos always publicize big wins and long runs of luck because they know these lovely stories will do two things: first, bring in new customers; and second, encourage them to ride their runs too long. In the romantic old game of roulette, for example, one of the popular even-money bets is *rouge ou noir,* red or black. The mathematical probabilities dealing with runs are exactly the same as in the case of a tossed coin. Every night in any active casino, short runs of red—three in a row, four in a row—happen hundreds of times. No casino ever troubles to publicize those. But on the rare occasions when a long run happens—ten or fifteen in a row—the casino's publicity office is sure to spread the news around.

In Monte Carlo once, red is supposed to have come up twenty-eight times in a row. The story may be apocryphal, but it is not inconceivable. Long runs, including fantastically long runs, *do* happen. But the point to keep in mind is that they happen rarely. If you insist on waiting for them, the strain on your gambling capital is going to be too great. You will go broke before your long run happens.

In probability law, you would have to spin a roulette wheel about 268 million times in order to have an even chance of seeing a run of twenty-eight reds. If you insisted on waiting for that run of twenty-eight, you would have to watch a lot of money go down the drain.

Of course it is nice to dream about betting on such a run and winning. If you started with a bet of ten dollars and let your money ride, so that it doubled with each coup or spin of the wheel, you would end the run of twenty-eight successful coups with an amount not far short of $1.5 billion. That is considerably more than the net worth of any casino in existence. Casino rules about the sizes of permissible bets would forbid such an outcome, but it certainly makes for a fun-filled fantasy.

On the other hand, if you let your money ride on red for the twenty-ninth coup, you would lose the whole $1.5 billion, including your original ten bucks.

The problem with runs of luck is that you never know how long they are going to last. When a run has begun, you cannot know in advance whether it will be a long one or will end with the next coup.

One thing you *can* know, however, is that short runs are very much more common than long ones. The sensible thing to do is ride the run until you have a good but not enormous gain, avoid greed, and get out early.

And don't fret if the run continues without you. Sometimes it will, and when it does, a few people will end up with very big gains; but in all likelihood they will turn around and lose those gains in short order, for they are not the kind of people who enjoy consistent good luck. The consistently lucky are the run cutters.

One of the oldest and wrongest pieces of advice you hear around Wall Street is "Cut your losses but let your profits ride." There is nothing wrong with the part about cutting losses. Indeed, we'll study that under the Fifth Technique: luck selection. But the last half of the old adage, the part about letting profits ride, is a recipe for bad luck.

Of course Wall Street is not a roulette wheel. If you are playing *rouge ou noir* and let your profits ride, you stand to lose everything instantly when the wrong color comes up. Runs of luck do not end so abruptly when you are speculating in stocks, real estate, rare coins, or other changeable-price entities that may attract you. They may end quite abruptly if you are heavily margined; that is, you finance your speculations with a lot of borrowed money. But if you are an ordinary cash speculator like most people, a downturn in the price of your stock or gold bullion won't necessarily bring total disaster. You don't lose your whole wad. You lose only the value off the top.

With that in mind, the old dictum about letting profits ride might sound like acceptable advice. You've bought a bundle of stock, we'll say. The company, Gee Whiz, is a manufacturer of doodads, thingamabobs, and other useful products, which your broker believes will sell well during the next twelve months. He shows you a lot of portentous-looking economic analyses to back up his view. So all right, you decide to take a chance and load up on Gee Whiz stock at ten dollars a share.

By sheer blind luck, your broker and his economic analysts turn out to be right. The stock price advances to fifteen dollars. You are in on a run of luck. What should you do?

"Let your profits ride," solemnly counsels the fellow across the hall at work. This chronic loser is so consistently unlucky that he can't even get out of a Friday night poker game without leaving all his pocket cash behind. He never had any profits and doesn't really understand what it might mean to let them ride. But he does have all the clichés committed to memory and can recite them in appropriately businesslike tones.

So you think: All right, I'll take the advice and ride this run of luck as far as it wants to take me. I'll ride it to its very peak! And when it tops out, I'll take my profit and run.

That is what you think. It sounds logical, and it sounds easy. It sounds particularly easy to the fellow across the hall, who never actually did it.

The fact is, however, that it is damnably hard. Indeed, for the majority it is so hard that it effectively is impossible.

What happens is that, having signed on for a long run, you work yourself into a psychological state in which nothing else will do. You trap yourself into waiting for the long run, which, nine times out of ten, isn't going to happen.

Very few people ever make money consistently on Wall Street, and my observations convince me this is one of the main reasons why, if not *the* reason. Beginners come into the market, hear that silly advice about letting profits ride, attempt to carry it out, get flattened, and finally withdraw in weary discouragement. They end up with their money in savings accounts and money market funds—which, as we've seen, is no way to get lucky.

The losing process typically begins with what could be a modest win or even a pretty good one. You're sitting there with your handful of Gee Whiz stock, which you bought at ten dollars a share. It jumped to fifteen dollars, then to twenty dollars. You've doubled your money! You really ought to be out of the game by now, but you're operating on the basis of letting profits ride. You have your sights set on a long run of luck. Maybe the price will go to thirty dollars, you think hopefully. You'll have tripled your money!

Unfortunately, the bottom drops out of the thingamabob market, and the price plunges back to fifteen dollars. You think: "This is just a temporary dip. I'll hang on until the runup resumes."

It doesn't. The price slumps to twelve dollars. You think: "This *must* be the end of the dip. It would be a mistake to sell out now and risk getting left behind. Suppose it quadruples? I'll kick myself!"

It doesn't quadruple, it sags to ten dollars, the price you paid for the stock. Now you're furious. You feel cheated. "I'll be *damned* if I'll let go of this now!" you tell yourself. "This stock owes me! I'm going to hang on until it pays off!"

So it collapses to five dollars.

And that is how losers are made. Bernard Baruch, a supremely lucky man, cut a lot of runs by selling all his stocks in the middle of a thundering bull market in 1928. He had made a lot of money and saw no good reason to go for more. Many speculators did go for more. Hanging on for longer runs, they all went down the drain in the crash that began in 1929.

Later in his life, Baruch was asked the question that all outstandingly lucky people are asked. What was the secret of his success? He replied, "Not being greedy."

# 7. The Fifth Technique: Luck Selection

"Cut your losses," they tell each other on Wall Street. Though few can do it well or consistently, it is still good advice. And it doesn't apply only to the stock market. It applies everywhere.

Florence Graham, better known by her business name, Elizabeth Arden, found herself dead-ended in her early thirties. She was employed as a clerk and beautician in a New York beauty salon. The years were slipping by, the pay was miserable, and the prospects for advancement were not encouraging. She wanted to quit and try something else. Friends argued with her: "You've invested a lot in that job. Why abandon it? Why lose what you've got? Stick around. Maybe it'll pay off if you give it time."

She faced a decision very much like that of a Wall Street investor with a sagging stock. Should she hold on and hope for an improvement in luck some day in an unknowable future? Or should she cut her losses right away, abandon the investment, and free herself to seek better luck somewhere else? She decided to cut her losses. She quit the job, opened a business of her own, and was a millionaire not many years later.

Lucky people have the knack of doing that, and it is one of the chief contributors to their good fortune. The knack is not easy to acquire. Wall Streeters often talk as though it is, and so do a lot of people like the fellow

77

across the hall, stuck for life in a mire of bad luck. If the knack were easy, a lot more people would have it and a lot more would be lucky. It isn't easy. I'm not going to kid you. But it is a knack you must acquire if you would be lucky.

As you enter any new venture—an investment, a job, a love affair— you cannot know how it will work out. No matter how carefully you lay your plans, you cannot know how those plans will be affected by the unforeseeable and uncontrollable events that we call luck. If the luck is good, then you stay with the venture and enjoy it. But what if the luck is bad? What if the bottom drops out of the stock market? Or the seemingly limitless promise of that new job vanishes in a corporate upheaval? Or your love affair sours when a rival suddenly appears?

The lucky reaction is to wait a short time and see if the problems can be fixed or will go away, and then, if the answer is no, bail out. Cut losses short. This is what lucky people habitually do. To put it another way, they have the ability to select their own luck. Hit with bad luck, they discard it, freeing themselves to seek better luck in another venture.

The unlucky, by contrast, are always getting themselves stuck— sometimes for life—in bad relationships and losing money ventures. They typically complain that fate has dealt them bad hands, but that usually isn't the problem. The unlucky receive no more bad hands, on an average, than anybody else. The difference is that the unlucky don't have the knack of selecting luck. Incapable of discarding a bad hand, they can only sit and suffer while bad luck becomes worse luck.

ONE REASON WHY luck selection is so difficult for most people is that it almost always involves the need to abandon part of an investment. The investment may be in the form of time, commitment, love, money, or something else. Whatever it is, you leave some of it behind when you discard a bad hand.

You buy a stock at one hundred dollars, and the price abruptly drops to ninety dollars. In the absence of compelling reasons to think the sag will reverse itself, you probably ought to cut your loss and sell out imme- diately. Only by doing that can you free your money to seek better luck in another investment. The problem is that the act of discarding this bad luck will require you to abandon part of your original one hundred-dollar investment. If you sell, you leave ten dollars behind.

For some, that is so hard that it is impossible. The unlucky investor talks himself out of it. "Things aren't as bad as they look! The price will go back up!" So he hangs on. The price drops to eighty dollars. Now he's stuck twice as hard. If he couldn't abandon ten dollars, how is he going to abandon twenty dollars? He is mired in his bad luck. Instead of having his money out chasing better luck elsewhere, he has allowed it to get trapped, perhaps for years.

Two psychiatrists, Stanley Block and Samuel Correnti, studied the "born loser" and reported on this unhappy breed in the book *Psyche, Sex and Stocks.* They found that the inability to abandon part of an investment is one of the loser's outstanding traits. Leaving part of oneself or one's money behind is an experience that troubles everybody to some extent, but the chronic loser is troubled more than other men and women.

The affliction is crippling. Unless the loser overcomes it, he is all but certain to remain a loser—and a loser not just in the investment world. This kind of person will get taken to the cleaner's in a poker game, for example. To be lucky in this game you *must* discard bad hands when you get them. This always means that you must leave some of your money behind in the pot, and it hurts—but you must do it or go broke. The loser cannot bear to do it. Instead, this unlucky player gets stuck with whatever unplayable hands fate and the dealer want to hand out.

The same loser is likely to get stuck in soured love affairs, for essentially the same reason. "I've given so much of myself to this relationship. I've worked at it so hard. All that time, energy and commitment—how can I just abandon it?"

And you often find the same loser trapped in job situations that have been hit by hard luck. Eric Wachtel, the management consultant and executive recruiter, observes that people will sometimes allow themselves to be trapped by concerns that are really quite trivial. "Pensions, for instance," Wachtel says. "I once approached a woman about a potentially terrific new career opportunity. It could have changed her life. She was going no place where she was. But she wasn't interested. She said, 'No, I've got X years invested in this job. Another couple of years and I'll qualify for a pension.' It wasn't much of a pension, but just because she wasn't willing to abandon it, she passed up a chance of a lifetime."

Wachtel reports that the woman remained dead-ended in the job he tried to lure her away from. Bad luck changed to worse luck. Her discouragement was reflected in her work, which grew careless. Finally she was fired. She undoubtedly felt bitter about her bad luck, but she could have discarded it.

ANOTHER REASON WHY luck selection is difficult for most is that it often requires a painful confession: "I was wrong."

To return to Wall Street for a simple example, let's say you've bought a stock at one hundred dollars, and it has slumped to ninety dollars. Obviously, buying it was a mistake. It was not by any measure a stupid mistake. Nobody can see the future. You can't, your broker can't, the president's economic advisers can't, and your five-year-old niece can't. To buy a stock or anything else whose price later slumps is not dumb; it is only a case of bad luck. But it *is* an error, and if you are going to cut your loss, you must admit that error to yourself, your broker, your spouse, and perhaps others.

For some, that is even harder to do than abandoning an investment. The loser's response is to seek excuses for not admitting the error. "I was right to buy this stock. Time will vindicate my judgment. The price will go back up. I'll come out looking smart in the end."

There is a trivial example of this difficulty that you have probably experienced many times in your life. You are in a car with your family or riding a bike with friends, heading for some unfamiliar destination. You come to a fork in the road. Lacking clear directions, you make a random choice. You ride for a while. It begins to become apparent that you have chosen the wrong route. At what point do you admit it?

Some would admit it fast and backtrack before a great deal of time is lost. Others, however, grimly drive on for miles. It hurts them that much to admit the error and discard the bad luck. Men seem more prone than women to this kind of difficulty behind the wheel of a car. Women's magazines enjoy publishing cartoons about that male quirk. But in other arenas of life, women have as much trouble as men in admitting error and getting out of a bad situation.

Getting out of a soured love affair is another example. A favorite theme of novelists for centuries has been that of a woman who ought to bail out of an affair but can't. Almost always, in fiction as in life, one part of the difficulty—one component of the trap—is an inability to say "I was wrong." Flaubert's Emma Bovary knows she should cut her losses and withdraw from the profitless affair with Leon, but she cannot make herself do it. Bad luck turns to worse luck, and in the end she kills herself with poison. Tolstoy's hapless Anna Karenina has similar hard luck in her affair with Count Vronsky. She finally chooses to end the long losing streak by throwing herself in front of a train.

Of course it is not as easy to bail out of a gone-wrong love affair as to reverse directions on a highway. There are degrees of difficulty in luck selection. Backtracking to correct a wrong choice of route is relatively easy for most. Selling a bad investment is harder. Quitting a disappointing job may be still harder. Backing out of a futureless love relationship may be the hardest and most complicated of all such loss-cutting acts.

But it is a technique you must practice if you seek good luck. Since you cannot see the future, there is only one way to find out what luck you will have in a given situation: enter the situation and see what happens. As we saw in our studies of the Third Technique, you *must* take risks. But with this Fifth Technique in your toolbox, you will always be ready to discard your luck if it turns out to be bad.

WE'VE TALKED ABOUT pessimism before, and we may find it useful now to take another look at this hard-to-define state of mind. Some problems involving pessimism may have been troubling you as you tried to come to grips with this difficult Fifth Technique.

In our studies of the Fourth Technique, run cutting, we noted that lucky people often seem to behave in a pessimistic way when dealing with runs and streaks of luck. Instead of hoping for long runs, they expect only

81

short ones. They habitually jump off before runs have reached their peaks.

Similar pessimism seems to be involved in luck selection. If an optimist buys a stock at one hundred dollars and it drops to ninety dollars, he is unperturbed—or at least pretends to be. "Oh, I don't care!" he says cheerfully. "The price will go back up! Everything will turn out all right in the end!" In the same situation, a pessimist is more likely to pick up the phone, call his broker and sell out.

Paradoxically, the pessimist's approach is more often the lucky one. The pessimist, habitually bailing out when hit with a 10 percent or 15 percent price drop, may suffer a string of small losses while waiting for a big gain. But he has two major advantages over the optimist. First, the pessimist can never get caught in a major crash. And second, he can never get his money stuck in a situation of long-term stagnation.

There are many speculators—in stocks, commodities, currencies—who sell out automatically on a 10 percent to 15 percent price drop. Such programmed selling appeals to some but not to others. Whether it is for you will depend on your temperament. However, it works only in the case of a speculative entity having a precisely known market price. There are many other areas of life and luck, of course, in which it isn't possible to arrive at such precise valuations. What is the value of a job? A love affair? How can you tell when its "price" has dropped 10 percent?

You cannot, of course. But you can tell when it has begun to turn sour. And when that happens, you can make use of the same healthy pessimism that serves the lucky speculator.

But now we had better pause and agree on what we mean by "pessimism." As used here, it doesn't refer to a state of chronic gloom, a long face, or a habit of expecting only bad things to happen. The kind of pessimism that characterizes the lucky is really a fairly cheery state. As we've noted before, "pessimism" may not be exactly the right word. "Realism" might be a little better. To define it as precisely as possible as it applies to the Fifth Technique, it is *the habit of avoiding unfounded optimism.*

Unfounded optimism is dangerous. On Wall Street, it is a killer. It is the habit or tendency to expect things to turn out well, even when there is no tangible reason to expect any such thing.

The lucky approach is to insist on seeing such evidence. Let's say you're in a career situation that has turned sour. Promises made when you were hired haven't been kept, or your mentor has retired early, or the company president's nephew has been moved in over your head. Bad luck has hit you. The "price" of the job has fallen. What do you do?

The unlucky optimist would cling to empty hope. "Things are bound to get better! I'll give it time. It'll all work out. Maybe it's all for the best. Things are never as bad as they seem!"

As a lucky realist, you would look at the situation differently. You would recognize, in the first place, that things usually *are* as bad as they seem. In fact, often they're worse. You would say to yourself, "I'm willing to be optimistic, but I've got to be shown some reasons why." And then you would study the situation. Is there some likelihood that the problems will go away? Or do you have some realistic hope of fixing them? If so, stay aboard. If not, get out and go looking for better luck elsewhere.

THIS FIFTH TECHNIQUE is without doubt *one* of the hardest techniques to master, and for some it is unequivocally *the* hardest. It is hard because it requires a kind of pessimism, or unsentimental realism, that doesn't come naturally to many. What makes it still harder is that there are times when, in retrospect, you wish you hadn't applied it.

You buy a stock for one hundred dollars. It sags to eighty-five dollars. You sell out. And then it soars to two hundred dollars. That hurts.

Or you quit a job that wasn't taking you anywhere. Unforeseen events then abruptly change the shape of the company. The person who took over your abandoned job gets boosted to astonishing heights of rank and pay. That hurts, too.

Or you're playing poker. Your hand is a probable loser, so you decide to cut your loss and fold. Watching the next cards fall, you observe that, against the odds, your hand would have taken the pot if you had stayed. Painful? Indeed.

But such dismaying outcomes do not happen often. Much more often, what starts to go wrong stays wrong—or goes wronger. In a souring situation, with no compelling reason to think things will get better, you are always right to cut your loss and go. You are right even when, in retrospect, you turn out to have been wrong.

Lucky people, as a breed, are able to live with the knowledge that some decisions will turn out wrong. This is part of their general habit of accepting risk. "You take risks going in and you take risks getting out," Bernard Baruch once said. "If you were to insist on 100 percent certainty, you would not be able to make any moves at all." So spoke an extremely lucky man.

# 8. The Sixth Technique: The Zigzag Path

It is a fundamental assumption of the Work Ethic that people ought to have goals and should struggle toward them in a straight line. We are counseled to fix our eyes on our goals, looking neither to the right nor to the left, refusing to be distracted. This is supposed to be the sure route to success.

But here is a puzzling fact. It turns out that lucky men and women, on the whole, are not straight-line strugglers. They not only permit themselves to be distracted, they *invite* distraction. Their lives are not straight lines but zigzags.

Goal orientation, as they call it in Psychology 101, is undoubtedly a good thing in moderate doses. But the lives of the lucky seem to say you should be wary of overdoing it.

LOOK AT MARY Garden, for example. She began her musical career by studying the violin. Then she switched to the piano. Then she took singing lessons. She attended some rehearsals of an opera in Paris and was in the opening-night audience, holding ticket number 113, when the star singer fell ill. Mary Garden was asked to fill in, and a new star was born.

Later in her life, she talked about goal orientation, as successful people often do. "I never lost sight of what I wanted to do," she claimed in her autobiography. But we would not know her name today if she hadn't lost sight of it at least twice. If she had not zigzagged, she would have kept her eyes fixed on the goal of becoming a violinist. By her own admission, she would probably not have been a very good one.

Or look at Harlan Sanders. He bounced around the world like a Ping-Pong ball before finding his big break. He dropped out of school in the seventh grade, worked at various menial jobs, collected fares on a streetcar, piloted a ferryboat, sold insurance, then went into the restaurant business. Largely by luck, he stumbled onto a recipe and method for turning out unusually tasty fried chicken on a mass-production basis. Colonel Sanders's Kentucky Fried Chicken quickly became a multi-million-dollar business.

Or take Ray Kroc. He, too, bounced around. A high school dropout, he started out with his eyes on the goal of a career in music. He played the piano in some traveling bands. Then he switched goals and made some money selling Florida real estate. Then music distracted him again, and he worked for a while as musical director of a radio station. A new selling opportunity distracted him next: He went on the road, selling paper cups. Another goal then loomed up to attract his roving gaze: the goal of having his own business. He set up as a manufacturer's representative, selling Multimixers—machines that mixed milk shakes.

And finally, after all that zigzagging, Ray Kroc hit the jackpot. One day, to his astonishment, he learned that a small California restaurant had eight of his Multimixers, far more than any other establishment. The restaurant was obviously doing a booming business. When his travels took him to the West Coast, Kroc made it a point to stop in at the restaurant and see what the big attraction was.

The attraction was a peculiarly delicious new version of an old American staple: hamburger and french fries. The restaurant's name was McDonald's.

Kroc knew a gold mine when he fell into one. He quickly formed a partnership with the two brothers who owned and operated the restaurant. Within a few years, under Kroc's management, the name McDonald's was celebrated across the nation and then around the world.

But Kroc, too, talked about goal orientation in his elder-statesman years. At the so-called "Hamburger University" in Elk Grove, Illinois, where prospective franchisees went to attend seminars dealing with the fast-foods business, Kroc would often give solemn Work Ethic preachments about the necessity of keeping one's eyes glued to one's goal. His speeches sounded uncannily like those of another great zigzagger, Tom Watson, the founder of IBM. Watson, too, liked to harangue students in company-operated schools. Except that Watson and Kroc were talking about two different products, their speeches were interchangeable. Both men stressed the need to crunch one's way through life in a straight line, never swerving, trampling down obstacles like a bulldozer.

Of course part of Kroc's motive in giving these speeches was that he didn't want his students swerving to goals outside McDonald's. But he seemed to genuinely believe that goal fixing is the route to success. Like Mary Garden, he appeared to forget that he owed his great good luck largely to the fact that he *hadn't* plodded toward a single, fixed goal as a younger man.

If Mary Garden and Ray Kroc had both been straight-line plodders, they might have met at some gathering of down-at-the-heels musicians. We can imagine the scene: They are two aging losers. She is eking out a living by giving violin lessons to bored teenagers, while he plays a dispirited piano in a band that hires itself out for dances and weddings, when it can get work at all.

"It's a tough business, Mary," he says morosely.

"Yes, but look at it this way, Ray," she says, trying to cheer him up. "No matter what happens, you've still got your music. That's always been the important thing for me. Having a goal to work toward!"

"Yeah, right!" he says, cheering up. "A goal!"

"Not like so many of these aimless young people nowadays."

"Right! Goals! We've got goals! Say, you don't suppose you could lend me ten bucks to tide me over till next week, could you?"

THE LUCKY, ALERT to the luck/planning distinction, are aware that life is always going to be a turbulent sea of opportunities drifting randomly past in all directions. If you put blinders on yourself so that you can see only straight ahead, you will miss nearly everything.

This is what the unlucky typically do. They stick to preplanned life routes even when they are going nowhere or are actually plodding downhill to disaster. "Oh, I wouldn't want to sell paper cups. I'm a pianist!" Thus speaks a potential loser. "Oh, I'm not interested in any new venture, I've got my life pretty well planned." Thus speaks another.

Long-range plans aren't actually harmful, but it is important not to take them seriously. A plan can be used as a kind of guide into the future but should never be allowed to harden into a law. If something better comes along, you should be ready to abandon your old plan immediately and without regret.

This is what the lucky are able to do. Typically, they do it without thinking about it much. As a breed, they instinctively avoid getting trapped in their own long-range plans.

"When I was younger," Elizabeth Arden told a *Fortune* reporter, "people chided me for not sticking with jobs long enough. It's a lucky thing I didn't."

It was indeed a lucky thing. She learned stenography and worked at that for a time. She held another job as a cashier. She worked as a dental assistant. At the age of thirty, she went to New York and got a job in a beauty salon. That was where, finally, she learned the trade that would make her famous.

Like Mary Garden and Ray Kroc, she became famous because she was willing to stay receptive to random bits of luck drifting past. She did not insist on plodding forward in a straight line. If something attractive bobbed up somewhere beside the trail she was traveling, she turned off the trail and started out in a new direction.

This doesn't mean you should make frequent changes just for the sake of change itself. It means only that if a piece of potential good luck drifts your way, you should not summarily reject it simply because it doesn't fit some predesigned plan.

If you do insist on following a plan, you are likely to end up playing the saddest game in the world—the game of "if only." This is a game played largely by losers in moments of lonely gloom. Looking back, they can identify turning points at which they could have made themselves into winners. Could have—*if only.*

"If only I'd gone into business with my two friends," lamented a middle-aged man one day at the New York Forty Plus Club. He was an industrial salesman specializing in computer software. That was the profession he had learned as a young starter, and it was the single track along which he had plodded throughout his career to date. The goal he had kept before him, in his words, was "to be the best damned software salesman in the business." That certainly sounds like a laudable goal. It would be applauded by all good Work Ethic fans. However, it had never done this poor wayfarer the slightest bit of good. After a long string of bad breaks, his job disappeared in a merger, and he was out on the sidewalk at the age of fifty-five.

He need not have been. Years back, two friends had approached him with an appealing suggestion. They were in the very first stages of founding a licensing agency. This was an enterprise that proposed to earn its living by representing sports personalities, TV stars, and other famous names. It would promote the use of these names in manufactured products such as clothing and toys, collecting commissions from the licensing fees paid by the manufacturers. The licensing business appeared to be growing rapidly, and the two entrepreneurs were able to paint a glowing picture in describing it to the computer man. They already had some business lined up, virtually guaranteeing a profitable first year for the infant enterprise. It was as nearly risk free as a new business can ever be. They wanted their friend, the computer man, to join them and take over certain marketing functions.

But he could not see in any direction but straight ahead. He was a software salesman, not a licensing agent, he protested. This new enterprise was off to one side of what he saw as his life's main street. And so he turned the opportunity down. He rejected a piece of potentially excellent luck that had drifted within his reach—rejected it without even studying it.

The licensing agency prospered in the middle 1980s, as most such agencies did. The computer man, left behind, could only stand there and say "if only."

*NEVER* TAKE LONG-range plans seriously. Use them for general guidance as long as they seem to be taking you where you want to go, but whatever you do, don't get stuck with them. Throw them in the trash heap as soon as something better comes along.

This approach or formula turns up again and again in the lives of the lucky. Most of them seem to follow it instinctively, without giving it much direct thought. They follow it because it *feels* right. But there are others who follow it in a more deliberate or cerebral way, as a thought-out philosophy.

An outstanding example is Helene von Damm, the United States ambassador to Austria through most of President Reagan's time in office. Mrs. von Damm's astoundingly lucky life is an advertisement for the value of the zigzag path, and she is keenly aware of the fact. She has always avoided long-range goals as a matter of deliberate personal policy.

"I don't belong to the people who make long-range plans," she told a *New York Times* reporter in 1985. "I like to take advantage of serendipity."

Serendipity, the faculty or habit of seizing lucky breaks that you weren't looking for, is another way of describing the zigzag life routes characteristic of lucky people. Helene von Damm's life has been the opposite of a straight line.

She was born poor in Austria in 1938. Her home village was occupied by the Russians after World War II. She was only a schoolgirl, but she understood quickly that life under the Soviets' own gray version of the Work Ethic was not for her. She watched for a chance to get out, and when one came, she got out. She fled to West Germany with hardly a pfennig in her purse. She found a job, but when she met an American soldier who wanted to marry her, she abandoned career goals instantly. She married the soldier and moved to Detroit.

Eventually, seeing other goals that attracted her more, she divorced the man. She found work, but then a more attractive secretarial job in

Chicago caught her eye, so she moved there. The main attraction of the new job was that it offered her a chance to circulate among interesting people instead of just sitting in a business office. The job was with a political-action committee of the American Medical Association.

In a short time she changed goals again. Her work for AMA put her in contact with an interesting man who had started adult life as an actor but now was zigzagging into politics. His name was Ronald Reagan. He asked the energetic and capable secretary to follow him home to California and work on his gubernatorial campaign. Quickly abandoning long-range AMA goals, she agreed.

She became Ronald Reagan's personal secretary, worked on his presidential campaign and followed him into the White House. In 1982 he named her ambassador to Austria, the country she had fled as a penniless emigrant many years before.

A life story that reads like a fairy tale. A story of amazing good luck. But Cinderella would never have made it to her happy ending unless she had always been ready to abandon old goals for new ones.

Never be afraid to zigzag. Avoid walling yourself into a category: "I'm a secretary. . . . I'm in the computer business. . . . I'm a Detroiter." You never know which direction your lucky breaks may come from. When they drift into reach, grab them.

# 9. The Seventh Technique: Constructive Supernaturalism

This technique is about religion and superstition. Those are two troublesome words. What's religion to me may be superstition to you, and vice versa. Many wars have been fought over differences of opinion concerning the two words, and huge quantities of nonsense have been generated in debates about them.

In our studies of luck, happily, we will be able to avoid those debates. We can lump religion and superstition together and refer to them by one neutral word: supernaturalism.

Supernaturalism is defined as any belief in an unseen spirit, force, or agency whose existence hasn't been proven to everybody's satisfaction.

It may be an absolutely serious belief such as orthodox Christianity or Judaism. It may be an occult science such as astrology or numerology. It may be something less serious, such as a fear of walking under ladders. It may be something quite trivial, such as a half-humorous fondness for a certain good-luck charm or a habit of knocking on wood to ward off bad luck.

All these are manifestations of supernaturalism. Whether serious or humorous, important to the believer or barely more than a kind of game or tic, they all fit the definition. All deal with unseen powers, and all can get you an argument at any cocktail party. All have adherents, and all have scoffers.

And all play a role in men's and women's varied approaches to the problem of getting lucky.

You will remember our definition of luck: events that influence your life but aren't of your making. Of whose making, then, are they? Ah, that is the question that causes all the trouble. It is the question that pits atheists against the pious, Moslems against Christians, astrologers against jeering multitudes, charm carriers and ladder dodgers against people who like the number 13.

You win a prize in a lottery. Why? Where did the good luck come from? What is its purpose? Why were you singled out to receive it? You have almost certainly asked yourself such questions at various times in your life. Everybody has. And there are dozens of possible answers.

God sent me the good luck for unknowable reasons.
God sent it because I prayed for it.
God sent it because I've been leading a blameless life.
It happened because it was ordained in my horoscope.
It happened because that was my lucky day.
It happened because the lottery ticket bore my lucky number.
I made it happen by wearing my good-luck bracelet.
I made it happen by finding a four-leaf clover and reciting my grand-
    mother's magic spell.

And so on. That is not by any means a complete list of supernatural explanations of luck. Some people favor one explanation to the exclusion of others. Some favor several. Some drift up and down the list, choosing the explanation to fit the given circumstances.

Finally, there are a large number of people who reject all supernatural explanations. These men and women might be called pragmatists. Their motto is: "I believe what I can see and touch." On winning a lottery prize they would be as happy as any of the supernaturalists, but their comments on the event would be cooler:

This good luck was not sent to me by any unseen spirit, force, or agency. It was simply a random event. Somebody had to win the prize, and the winner chanced to be me. My good fortune has no purpose; nor does it prove anything. It just *happened.*

We now come to the core question. Are lucky people supernaturalists or pragmatists?

They are both—but in a special way. And that will take some explaining.

LUCK THEORY, THE body of advice that is the basis of this book, is entirely pragmatic in its essential nature. It reckons without supernatural forces of any kind. Even this Seventh Technique, as you will see, takes an agnostic attitude toward religious and occult beliefs. The other twelve techniques ignore those beliefs entirely. In basic luck theory, you can apply the techniques without prayer, horoscopes, lucky numbers, four-leaf clovers, or any other reliance on the supernatural.

You can. But that doesn't mean you must.

The techniques work with or without the supernatural. If you harbor a strong religious or occult belief, there is no reason why you can't remain true to that belief while applying the techniques. The same goes for supernatural tics and quirks: a fear of black cats, an aversion to the number 13, a half-humorous belief in the luck-bringing powers of a rabbit's-foot key ring. The thirteen techniques of luck theory are compatible with all supernatural beliefs and schema.

To put it another way, it shouldn't matter much in luck theory whether you believe in God or a committee of gods, or lucky numbers, or stars—or nothing. But here is a peculiar fact. As a breed, lucky people tend to be supernaturalists. Some are devoutly religious, while others harbor occult beliefs or enjoy playing humorously with supernatural formulas.

This baffled me when I first began to notice it. Why should the lucky be associated with supernaturalism?

What baffled me all the more at first was that it didn't seem to matter *which* brand of supernaturalism a lucky man or woman espoused. Some of the lucky are devout Catholics or Jews, while other shun religion but are dedicated to astrology or Tarot cards. What seems to be important isn't the *kind* of supernaturalism, but the fact that it is there at all. Nearly all lucky people, it turns out, associate themselves in some way with some kind of religious or occult idea.

What is the connection? The connection is that a supernatural belief, even a trivial and humorous one, helps people get lucky by helping them make otherwise impossible choices.

Life is full of situations in which you must choose among alternatives but lack any rational basis for choosing. The simplest illustration is that of number picking at Las Vegas or in your state lottery. You want to bet on a roulette wheel or in the state's three-digit game. To bet, you must choose a number to put your money on, but how? One number is just as good as another. No amount of cogitation is going to help you. No amount of figuring out will give you the slightest edge over other players. So what do you do?

Many people—the unlucky—would just stand there paralyzed, unable to make the impossible choice. But we saw in our studies of the Third Technique, risk spooning, that getting lucky requires taking risks. We also saw that we rarely have all the facts we could wish for when embarking on a risky course, and sometimes we have no facts at all. This is where the lucky can make a supernatural belief pay off.

The lucky man or woman would place that lottery bet despite the total lack of relevant data. How to pick the number? By relying on the supernatural.

The reliance might be perfectly serious: "God will guide me." Or it might be only partly serious: "My horoscope says good fortune will come to me from Scorpio people this week, so I'll find a Scorpio and ask her to suggest a number." Or it might be altogether humorous: "I'll kiss my lucky charm and pick the first three numbers that pop into my head."

Thus does the lucky individual get into the game. Whether the outcome is affected by God, the stars, or a lucky charm is irrelevant. What counts is that the supernatural belief has enabled the player to get into a potentially winning position.

Entering a lottery is a trivial adventure, of course. Life presents us with many more important fork-in-the-road situations. Some are just as frustrating as the lottery, in that no rational choice is possible. Yet the worst reaction of all is to do nothing.

A classic illustration of this common human dilemma is Frank Stockton's irritating story about the lady and the tiger. Maybe you remember it. The hero, having incurred the anger of a king, is led into a stadium that has two exit doors. Behind one door is a lady; behind the other, a tiger that has not enjoyed a good meal in a long time. The king tells the hero he must walk out through one door or the other. If he does not, he will be executed on the spot.

While the hero is pondering this interesting dilemma, the problem is compounded by his lover, the king's daughter. The princess surreptitiously points to one of the two doors. Unfortunately, he cannot figure out what her motivation might be. If she is motivated by selfless love for him, then she must be indicating the door with the lady behind it. But if she is motivated by jealousy, then she is steering him to the tiger.

A classic case of inadequate data. No amount of figuring is going to lead the baffled hero to a solution. No rational choice is possible. Yet the worst reaction is to stand there and do nothing, for that will bring certain execution. It is clearly to the hero's advantage to pick a door. In that way he gains a fifty-fifty chance of survival.

Stockton does not tell us the outcome. But we can hope, for the hero's sake, that he harbored a supernatural belief. Any old superstition would do, any occult discipline, any religion—just as long as he had *something* to guide him in the choice he had to make. Anything—even the ancient ritual of tossing a coin—would have been better than failing to make the choice.

Real life abounds with examples of similar dilemmas: frustrating situations in which we must make choices and take risks without nearly enough data. A Union Carbide executive tells the sad story of a young man who was unable to choose between two jobs.

He was an unusually bright young man with an excellent educational record. In his senior year at college he talked to recruiters sent to the campus to represent several large companies, among them Union Carbide and IBM. The recruiters found him somewhat lacking in personal grace and other attributes but were impressed by his intellect. Union Carbide and IBM ended up offering him virtually identical jobs.

He studied the offers, and he studied the companies, and he thought and thought, but he couldn't decide. He was in a pickle very much like that of the man in Frank Stockton's tale. No amount of cerebration could help him arrive at a choice. Union Carbide and IBM are both very large companies with well-earned reputations for generosity to employees. A bright young man or woman can have a wide-open future in either organization. But of course one's future in such an organization, like all futures everywhere, depends largely on luck. It is impossible to stand at the beginning of such a future and determine exactly what its shape is going to be. There are not enough data.

The young recruit couldn't make up his mind. Union Carbide personnel people wrote to him and then phoned him to say they had to have his decision soon. If he didn't want the offered job, they would like to offer it to somebody else. It was a good job. There was no shortage of qualified applicants. So what was it to be—yes or no?

IBM was undoubtedly prodding him for a decision in the same way as Stockton's hero. He was in a situation in which the worst choice would be to make no choice.

Finally, goaded to reluctant action by insistent letters and calls from the two huge companies, he told a Union Carbide woman on the phone that he had decided to go with IBM. The Union Carbide executive who tells this story isn't sure about just what happened at IBM, but apparently, there was a misunderstanding. When the young man went to notify IBM of his decision, the IBM people said they were sorry, but he had delayed too long. They had offered the job to another applicant, who had accepted it immediately. The young man called Union Carbide, but now that job was gone, too.

This was clearly a case in which the supernatural could have led to good luck. If the young man had harbored a religious belief, for example, he might have prayed for guidance or a sign or omen. Or he might have talked with a minister, rabbi, priest, or other guru. Or he could have sought guidance from a deck of Tarot cards or a horoscope. All he needed was *something* to lead him to a choice. No matter how silly or superstitious that something might appear to nonbelievers, it would have been of direct practical value if it had helped the young man overcome his paralysis.

SO FIND YOURSELF a supernatural guidance system. It can be serious or humorous, a profoundly held belief or a game. None of that matters. Nor does it matter whether the system, in terms of its pronouncements about itself, is "true" or is pure poppycock. All that matters is that you hold it and can use it to help you make choices and take risks.

Don't be afraid of seizing a system that others scoff at. *All* supernatural systems get scoffed at, including the major religions. Nobody knows whether the truth about God and the world is perceived by Christians, Jews, Moslems, or somebody else—or nobody. A lot of people *say* they know, but they don't; they only hope. Not everybody is convinced, indeed, that there is such a being as God or that, if there is, he or she cares who wins lotteries or gets jobs.

But in luck theory it doesn't matter.

It's the same with astrology. Are human affairs influenced by the positions of stars and planets? I don't know, anymore than I know whether there is a God. I personally doubt it, but that doesn't matter. What matters is that God and astrology are two supernatural belief systems that can help you get lucky, should you choose either or both.

There is a wonderful cornucopia of other choices. The Tarot is a lot of fun, though complicated. Almost any medium-sized library will provide you with books explaining how to divine the future and arrive at choices by means of Tarot readings. The images on Tarot cards and their combinations are peculiarly compelling and are also directly relevant to questions of luck. Many Tarot devotees get as thoroughly absorbed in their supernatural belief as priests and rabbis get in theirs. If that happens to you, it probably won't do you any harm.

Numerology is also fun, and it has the virtue of being simpler than most other occult or religious disciplines. It can be complicated if you want it to be, but it can be reduced to the simple act of espousing one or a few lucky numbers. Largely for that reason, it is my personal choice as a supernatural aid to luck.

I am fond of the numbers 6 and 28. They are the numbers that represent my birthday, June 28. They are also the only two "perfect" whole numbers below 100. In number theory, a perfect number is one that is the sum of its own factors. Thus the factors of 6 are 1, 2, and 3, which add up to 6.

So 6 and 28 are obviously rare and admirable numbers. Do I take them seriously? Of course not. But they do help me make choices in situations in which there is no rational basis for choice, and the worst course would be to stand there and do nothing.

For example, not long ago, while driving my car on my way to an unfamiliar destination, I came to a traffic circle with roads radiating out from it at crazy angles. I didn't know where I was or which road I should take. But I knew I had to make a choice and do it fast. If I were simply to stop dead in the midst of the traffic, paralyzed with indecision, I would not live long. I had to make my choice even though I had no data to base it on.

In this frustrating and potentially dangerous situation, my lucky number 6 came to my aid. On one of the roads I saw a service station with a tall sign advertising a brand of gasoline: Phillips 66. Without another moment's thought I turned down that road.

I got to my destination. I learned later that I hadn't chosen the shortest route, but I did get where I was going, and I lived to tell the story.

In much the same way those lucky numbers have helped me pick lottery numbers, play roulette wheels, even make decisions in data-lacking situations on the stock market. Sometimes I win and sometimes I lose. Except in playful moments, I doubt that the numbers have any effect on these outcomes. What the numbers *do* do for me is get me into the games—games I might otherwise shun because there is no way to figure out a rational winning strategy. The numbers help me put myself in position to win. And because I keep putting myself in position, I win often enough to make unlucky people jealous.

IF YOU ARE not attracted to any of the standard religious or occult systems, simply invent your own. One way to do this is to take a standard system and modify it to your taste.

There are millions of people who adhere in a general way to Christianity or Judaism, for example, but take no part in traditional observance. They belong to no churches or synagogues, have no interest in the Sunday or Sabbath rituals, and find the Bible long-winded and boring. Still they feel themselves to be good Christians or Jews. They can feel this way because they have been able to modify the religion to suit their personal tastes. They have simplified it, pared down the rituals, reduced the demands.

Any good minister, priest, or rabbi will tell you that you aren't supposed to do this. You can't just take a religion and remodel it to suit yourself, the gurus will insist. But of course, you can. Religion is personal. You can conduct your religious life in any way you want to conduct it.

It's the same with astrology, witchcraft, or the Tarot. All these occult systems are complicated and difficult if you adhere strictly to the traditional teachings. Many people enjoy the long, careful rituals and meticulously exact formulas. If that is the case with you, fine. An occult system like the Tarot can become an absorbing and richly rewarding hobby—or far more than a hobby: a religion. But if, on the other hand, you would prefer not to invest a great deal of time, effort, or emotional commitment in any such belief, then you can modify it to suit yourself.

Astrology, for instance, can be reduced to the simple sun-sign formulations of a daily newspaper horoscope. The Tarot, gorgeously complex when you lay out all seventy-eight cards of the deck, can be radically simplified by various approaches in which you consult only half a dozen cards or only one.

Numerology is similarly adaptable. I like it bare-bones simple, being unwilling to put a lot of work into it. But there are others who derive enjoyment from complex numerical relationships and structures. They are fascinated by magic squares and numerical palindromes, whose very complexity is felt to be part of their charm and also part of their luck-producing magic.

A Swiss bank executive of my acquaintance, for example, uses magic squares to help him in data-lacking situations in his personal gold and currency speculations. One icon of his religion is a stunningly intricate structure called a hypermagic square of the eighth order. Another is the Rookwise Square of Euler, a thing of shining symmetry and supposedly awesome magic powers.

Such hard-working supernaturalism may appeal to you. Or you may be content, instead, with the easiest supernaturalism of all: carrying or keeping a lucky charm. You will be in good company. Arlene Francis carries a lucky pendant, wearing it under her clothes if it doesn't go with her outfit. Zsa Zsa Gabor is never far from a child's ring given to her by her grandmother. With Johnny Carson it's a pair of mismatched cuff links. This supernatural tic was established when he lost one of a matched pair just before his first successful "Tonight" show in 1962. He went on the air with a borrowed link in one cuff and could never get out of the habit. These are all examples of constructive supernaturalism.

"A superstition won't do you any harm as long as you don't use it as a substitute for thinking," said Charles Goren, the bridge master. He was talking to a group of reporters and was responding to a question about bridge superstitions, specifically the one about bathtubs. "In fact, a superstition can help you. If it makes you feel good to sit facing in a certain direction, then probably you'll play better. You'll get up from the table with the feeling that you improved your luck."

The feeling would almost certainly be accurate. In bridge as in life, your fate is influenced by events beyond your control, particularly by the way the cards fall in the deal. You are stuck with the hand you pick up: thirteen cards not of your choosing. But these thirteen strokes of luck, good or bad or ho hum, are not the sole determinants of your fate. The game's outcome will also be influenced by what you do with the luck you are handed. With a good superstition to help you take risks and make data-short decisions, you are likely to be luckier than if you simply sat there baffled and discouraged.

Asked whether he harbored a supernatural luck-changing belief of his own, Goren grinned and nodded. He would not say what his belief was, but it did not matter. What counted was that he had *something* supernatural to lean on when he needed it. Charles Goren was always a supremely lucky man.

# 10. The Eighth Technique: Worst-Case Analysis

We've noted before that the lucky, as a breed, tend to be pessimistic. They certainly don't fit the image suggested by the funny old phrase "happy-go-lucky." That phrase conjures up a picture of a breezily optimistic, carefree man or woman who never worries about bad outcomes. The paradoxical fact is that such people, despite their cheery smiles and sunny dispositions, usually lead unlucky lives.

Optimism means expecting the best, but good luck involves knowing how you will handle the worst.

Entering any new situation—a job, a personal relationship, a money venture—the lucky person applies the First Technique. He or she makes a clear distinction between planning and luck: "This situation is only partly under my control. Good or bad luck—events not of my making—could make it ripen into something good or could make it go sour." Having fixed that in mind, the lucky individual then applies a worst-case analysis.

"I know this situation can go wrong. Now I've got to ask *how* it can go wrong. What is the worst possible outcome? Or if there are two or more 'worst' outcomes, what are they? How can it go wrongest? And if the worst does happen, what will I do to save myself?"

That is the opposite of being happy-go-lucky.

Margaret Farrar was among the very luckiest of all the people I've ever

103

interviewed, and she owed a good deal of her stunning success to the fact that she was a dedicated worst-case analyst. Let's take a look at her long, happy life.

She lived in the world of crossword puzzles, and for many years she was its undisputed queen. She all but invented crosswords as we now know them, worked for twenty-seven years as crossword editor of *The New York Times,* and turned out a fabulously profitable series of puzzle books for Simon and Schuster. But the likelihood is that we would not know her name today if she had not applied this Eighth Technique at least twice in her lucky career.

I went to see her in 1979. She lived in a large, old, book-cluttered apartment on New York's Upper East Side. She met me at the door: a small, trim woman of eighty-two with a brisk, friendly manner. I had not come to interview her specifically on the subject of luck, but I knew immediately that I was in the presence of a consistently lucky personality. After she had given me a cup of coffee, she began to tell me her life story with these words: "Succeeding at anything isn't just a matter of being smart, you know. You've got to be lucky, too." (That was the First Technique in action.) "I've always been lucky. It started when I was a young woman. I always seemed to be in the right places at the right times."

Margaret Farrar—then known either by her maiden name, Petherbridge, or her nickname, Piff—turned up in New York in 1921. After bouncing around a bit, she found a job as secretary to the Sunday editor of the old *New York World.*

The *World* had recently begun publishing what it called "word cross puzzles" to fill space. These were uninteresting little diamond-shaped constructions containing no words longer than six letters. Neither the editors nor the readers had much enthusiasm for them. They were regarded as mere space fillers and that attitude showed. The puzzles were marred by errors, made-up words such as "xinx" (defined as "sound made by falling coins"), dull definitions, and a general lack of pride and care.

The job of producing the weekly puzzle was assigned to junior staff members, none of whom wanted it. Each would perform the task ill-temperedly for a few weeks, then think of a reason why it should be dumped into the lap of somebody else. Finally, it was Piff Petherbridge's turn.

When an editor asked her to take on the job, her first reaction was delight. She guessed—more correctly than she knew, as it turned out—that a piece of unexpected good luck had come blundering into her life. "I saw it as a way to escape the secretary trap," she recalled. "In those days, secretarial jobs trapped most women all through their working lives. If you were a woman and you got a chance to do something else, *anything else*, you went for it."

But when that first surge of euphoria subsided, young Piff applied the indispensable Eighth Technique. She asked what could go wrong, and a very gloomy scenario presented itself to her. She saw herself devoting full time to the puzzle in order to improve it. The improvements would happen slowly. The general lack of enthusiasm would remain. Finally, the editors would decide to abandon the puzzle. Piff would want to return to her secretarial job, but somebody else would be filling it. And so Piff would find herself out on the sidewalk.

That was the worst case as she imagined it. She made her worries known to an editor, who laughed and said she was inventing nightmares. Nonetheless, she insisted on extracting a promise from the editor. The promise was that the *World* would continue publishing the puzzles for at least a year no matter what happened.

If young Piff had not applied this worst-case analysis and arranged protection for herself, it is conceivable that crossword puzzles as we know them today would not exist.

She began her new assignment with high enthusiasm. She expanded the puzzles' size so as to offer more challenge for literate readers. She tightened the rules under which the puzzles were constructed. She discouraged use of unfamiliar words such as "fiber of the gomuti palm" (which had appeared in the first puzzle the *World* ever published) where a more common word could be substituted with a little thought. She discouraged other lazy tricks such as making up a word like "xinx." She also tightened the editing and proofreading so as to eliminate misspellings, definitions keyed with the wrong numbers, and other errors. And she paid special attention to the patterns of blacked-out squares. She established rules that have since become gospel in American puzzledom (though not in England): The pattern must have an eye-pleasing symmetry; every letter must be part of two words; and so on.

But, as she had foreseen in her worst-case scenario, there was no instant surge of enthusiasm for the puzzles. Some of the newspaper's top editors decided that "word cross puzzles" were never going to be of any help in building circulation. They wanted to abandon the puzzles.

But Piff Petherbridge held them to their promise: one year. As it turned out, that gave her just enough time. By the end of the year, readers' enthusiasm had risen just enough to persuade the editors that they should continue publishing puzzles for another few months. And so the young puzzle editor's lifelong enterprise was saved.

In time, the crosswords became one of the *World*'s most popular daily features. Piff's tiny empire grew when two young assistant editors joined her.

Then, in 1924, crossword puzzles suddenly became a national craze. It came about when two smiling young men were escorted to Miss Petherbridge's desk. Their names were Richard Simon and Max Schuster. They had a harebrained scheme in mind. They wanted to start a publishing company, and they thought they would like to launch the venture by publishing a book of crossword puzzles. They wanted the *World*'s puzzle editor and her assistants to put the book together.

The newspaper's top columnist, Franklin P. Adams, advised her not to touch the scheme with a ten-foot pole. It couldn't succeed, he said. Crossword puzzles were an esoteric pastime for a very small, select group of quirkily literate people. To hope that a puzzle book would appeal to a mass market was ridiculous.

But the fledgling firm of Simon and Schuster was offering the puzzle editors twenty-five dollars apiece to assemble the proposed book. Piff could think of many good uses for twenty-five dollars. Moreover, when she subjected the situation to a worst-case analysis, it did not look very bad. "Suppose the book failed," she said, explaining her reasoning. "Suppose it failed *miserably*. What would I lose? My good name? But I really had very little of a name to lose at that point."

She decided the situation was much like that of entering a lottery: The risk of losing was large, but the amount to be lost was small. Just in case the book did succeed, she negotiated a contract under which she would share in the financial rewards through royalties.

She and her assistants began to assemble the book. But now a different "worst case" presented itself to her. Suppose the manuscript got lost?

Some *World* editors ridiculed this private nightmare of hers, but she had thought about it carefully. What started her worrying about it was a steady ebbing of enthusiasm for the book. There had never been high enthusiasm to begin with, but even that modest allotment was diminishing. Franklin P. Adams had refused to write a foreword. So had several other prominent literary folk, including the well-known editor and literary critic, John Farrar. Faced with this repeated rejection, Simon and Schuster were beginning to have second thoughts. Maybe a crossword book wasn't such a good idea after all.

Piff sensed that it would take only one more misfortune to induce them to abandon the project. It wouldn't have to be a major misfortune. Any minor stroke of bad luck would do. One possible stroke of bad luck, as she analyzed it, could be the loss of the manuscript.

If she lost it, she could reconstruct it, but that might take a month or two. She would then fail to meet Simon and Schuster's deadline. That failure, added to the continuing decline of general enthusiasm, might bring on the death of the project. She could hear Simon saying to Schuster, "You mean we've got to wait two more months for this book? Listen, maybe this is a blessing in disguise. I've been thinking for a long time that we ought to talk this over." And she could hear Schuster saying to Simon, "Well, yes, since you mention it, I've been having some second thoughts myself."

When she asked them directly if they were losing enthusiasm, they tried to assure her they were not. She strongly suspected that was only a kindhearted lie. She became sure of it when they announced a change of plan. Instead of issuing the book under the name they had originally chosen for their company, Simon and Schuster, they planned to dissociate themselves from possible failure by hiding behind the name Plaza Publishing.

This piece of news intensified Piff's worries about losing the manuscript. There were no copying machines in those days; and while carbon paper was available, few newspaper people ever used it. As a result, there was only one complete copy of the crossword book. The three editors added to it piece by piece, sometimes taking parts of it home, often leaving it lying about on desks and file cabinets. There were too many ways in which all or part of it could get lost. Piff spent two weekends making a complete copy by hand.

And just as she had foreseen in her worst-case scenario, the original manuscript got lost. Somebody left it in a cab. Since the publishers' deadline was only a week or two away, that could have been the end of the project. Also the end of Piff's bright and lucky future. But she had taken steps to save herself. She turned in the duplicate manuscript. And, thus, she preserved the good luck that might otherwise have fluttered out of her grasp.

The book was published on April 10, 1924. Price: $1.35, including a pencil, an eraser, and a postcard that could be mailed to Plaza Publishing for a set of puzzle solutions.

The first printing was a timid and pessimistic 3,600 copies. To everybody's surprise, it sold out instantly. Something about crossword puzzles seemed to have touched an American nerve. A second printing also sold out. So did a third and larger printing, and so did a series of progressively bigger ones, up to an eighth, ninth, and tenth of twenty-five thousand copies each. Before that astounding and crossword-mad year was over, two more puzzle books had been rushed into print. On a single day during the Christmas shopping season, some 150,000 were sold.

Piff Petherbridge was rich. She was soon to marry the contrite literary critic who had refused to write a foreword for her first book, and as Margaret Farrar she would quickly become famous throughout the English-speaking world. When Webster's New International Dictionary installed the phrase "crossword puzzle" as a regular listing for the first time in 1934, Margaret Farrar was asked for a ruling on whether or not the spelling should include a hyphen. When *The New York Times* instituted its first Sunday puzzle in 1942, she was hired as editor, and she oversaw the inauguration of the first daily puzzle in 1950. She was the queen of crossword puzzledom and remained queen throughout her life.

"I wasn't unusually clever or unusually anything," she would say. "I was just lucky." Exactly. Composing and editing crossword puzzles requires a high degree of literacy and a lot of patience, but there are thousands of people who are abundantly supplied with these good qualities. Margaret Farrar became the ruler of puzzledom because she was in the right place at the right time—and because, at least twice, she applied the Eighth Technique.

She asked what the worst outcome could be and prepared herself to handle it. If she had been happy-go-lucky instead, her great good luck would not have happened.

WE ARE NOW in a position to ask a question that has baffled amateur gamblers for centuries: *Why do professionals usually win?*

"Because they cheat," is the cliché reply, but the truth is that professionals—meaning men and women who earn all or a substantial part of their income by gambling—are far less likely to cheat than amateurs are. Cheating would be foolish for a pro. The pro doesn't need to take that extra risk.

Professional gamblers win because they reject optimism. They apply the Fifth Technique: the trick of selecting luck, of abandoning any venture rapidly when it turns sour. And they apply the Eighth Technique: the trick of worst-case analysis.

The amateur gambler hopes or prays the cards will fall his way. That is optimism, and it doesn't win card games. The pro, by contrast, studies how he will save himself when the cards fall against him.

That is the single most important reason why pros almost always go home with more money in their pockets than amateurs do. And it is the same on Wall Street. If you analyze the differences between consistent winners and losers in that greatest of all gambling casinos, one difference stands out starkly: The losers are optimistic.

*The New York Times* once sent a reporter around to interview a commodities speculator named Martin Schwartz, a consistent winner who in one year increased his fortune by a spectacular 175 percent. Asked how, Schwartz said succinctly, "I learned how to lose."

# 11. The Ninth Technique: The Closed Mouth

Calvin Coolidge, our twenty-ninth president, was noted for his habit of keeping his thoughts to himself. People called him "Silent Cal." Some—particularly those who didn't like his conservative, business-oriented political leanings—suggested that the reason why he didn't say much was that he didn't think much. But it is most unlikely that that was true. The evidence is that Calvin Coolidge, a man who enjoyed uncommonly good luck all through his life, understood or intuitively felt that unnecessary talk can become a barrier against lucky breaks.

As we've noted many times in this book, our paths through life are determined to a great extent by events not of our making, which is our definition of luck. We cannot control the flow of these events nor predict what they will be. But we *can* know that they are going to occur. Time and again, we are going to be dealing with the unexpected. That being so, the best strategy would seem to be one of maximum flexibility: keeping ourselves free to deal with those unknowable events in whatever ways seem appropriate at the time.

The trouble with too much talk is that it can constrict that valuable freedom and flexibility. Talk can tie you up, lock you into positions that seem right today but may be wrong tomorrow.

"I have often regretted my speech, but never my silence," wrote

111

Publilius Syrus, a Roman author of mimes and aphorisms who flourished in the first century B.C. He may have been referring simply to the morning-after regret that has been familiar to men and women through all the ages: "Oh God, did I really tell *that* story?" But it is more likely Publilius was thinking about the kind of regret that seizes you when an unexpected shift of events leaves you stranded.

"I've never liked Marie much," you confide to a group one day. The next day, in one of those unpredictable shifts, Marie finds herself in a position to direct a lucky break your way. Why didn't you keep your mouth shut?

"I wouldn't work for that company no matter how much they paid me," you declare. Those are words that you may one day wish you had never spoken.

"I'm uncomfortable dealing with people like him."

"I think they did a pretty poor job of organizing that project."

As Publilius Syrus knew, words can come back to haunt you. Silence almost never does.

This doesn't mean you must turn yourself into a stone statue. Fast-flow orientation requires you to be in contact with a lot of people, and that requires talk. Moreover, there are times when events force you to take positions and state views strongly. The lesson of this Ninth Technique is that the luckiest people guard against *unnecessary* talk. They are particularly careful when talking of subjects that have great personal importance to them. They reveal no more of their thinking than they have to. They don't lock themselves into positions when there is no good reason to do so.

Typically, others think of them as somewhat mysterious. "I never really know what's going through her head." And that is as it should be.

CALVIN COOLIDGE LIVED in an era that was almost as talky as ours. He was by no means a stone statue, but he did shun unnecessary jabber, and that made him stand out. He became the subject of caricatures. A motor-mouthed Washington hostess reportedly buttonholed him one evening and gushed, "I do hope you'll talk to me, Mr. Coolidge! A friend bet me I

112

wouldn't get more than two words out of you!" Coolidge replied coolly, "You lose."

He wasn't really that silent. No man so taciturn could have used the fast flow as successfully as Coolidge did. He talked enough to attract the lucky breaks he needed. Starting adult life as an obscure young lawyer in Northampton, Massachusetts, in 1898, he took exactly twenty-five years to become president of the United States. He did it by moving quickly, smoothly, and almost effortlessly through successively higher positions: mayor, state senator, governor, vice president, president. He never lost an election, and this astonished people. "There was a certain inevitability about the way he moved ahead," wrote his wife's awe-struck biographer, Ishbel Ross, "without seeming to exert himself unduly or beat the drums."

He didn't often need to exert himself because his acquaintanceship network did much of the work for him. He was always in the right place at the right time. Though there is no record that he ever used a term such as "fast flow," he must have realized in thinking about his life that he owed his continuing success mostly to the very big network of contacts he had established.

The "Coolidge luck" was almost as much talked about as was his parsimony with words. When he was elected vice president of the United States in 1920, his young law partner, Ralph Hemenway, cracked a joke that turned out to be grimly prophetic. "With your luck," Hemenway said, "I wouldn't want to be in the president's shoes." Three years later President Warren Harding died in office, and Coolidge succeeded him.

It troubled Coolidge that some of his most important lucky breaks depended on other people's bad luck. He may even have owed his life to such a break. In 1915, shortly after he was nominated for the office of Massachusetts lieutenant governor, he was knocked over by a car while crossing a street. The impact hurled him against a woman, and he fell on top of her. Because of that cushioned landing he was able to get up with only some trivial bruises, but the unfortunate woman sustained more serious injuries, including a broken arm.

But that kind of luck is blind, random, and uncontrollable. There is nothing sensible to be said or done about it. The main threads of explainable luck in Coolidge' life came from his acquaintanceship network and his frugality with words.

According to Ishbel Ross, Coolidge's philosophy was expressed in a snatch of doggerel that he had framed and hung over his mantel when he was mayor of Northampton:

> A wise old owl sat on an oak.
> The more he saw, the less he spoke.
> The less he spoke, the more he heard.
> Why can't we be like that old bird?

Great poetry it wasn't. And there is some evidence that Coolidge's gregarious wife, Grace, regarded this snippet of middlebrow parlor furnishing with considerable distaste. But it did sum up one of the major reasons for Coolidge's lifelong good luck.

People liked silent Cal, and in this fact lies one lesson of the Ninth Technique: You don't have to have your mouth going all the time to establish a circle of good friends and a widespread acquaintanceship network. As a matter of fact, in a talky time such as the present, people often find silence pleasantly surprising and refreshing. You can make friends as easily by listening, really *listening,* as you can by generating great heaps of words. Indeed, nonstop talk can irritate people—especially those who wish to be nonstop talkers themselves.

People not only liked Coolidge but were intrigued by the mystery of the man. What was he thinking? Nobody knew, except on the rare occasions when he chose to tell them. And because of this frugality with words, he preserved the freedom to react flexibly to unexpected events and turn them into strokes of good luck.

The event that hurled him to national prominence was a strike by the Boston police in 1919, while he was Massachusetts governor. Coolidge had never talked much about his views on unionization of public employees. When the threat of a strike boiled up suddenly, he warned the union leaders that he would not tolerate a police walkout, but they chose not to believe him. It was a serious miscalculation. To their astonishment, the inscrutable governor threw the full weight of his authority against the strikers—and, still worse for them, made a national issue of it by deliberately getting into a public debate with Samuel Gompers, the president of the American Federation of Labor.

"There is no right to strike against the public safety by anybody, anywhere, anytime," Coolidge declared flatly, and the majority of the U.S. press and public cheered. From that moment on, Calvin Coolidge was on his way to the presidency.

It was a fine example of how to seize an unexpected event and turn it to good fortune. Coolidge was able to do this because he had kept himself free. He had not done a lot of talking. He had not aligned himself unnecessarily with groups and positions, only to find that he had to do a lot of wiggling to get free. When the potentially lucky event occurred, he *was* free.

The event required that he take a position, and he did—unequivocally. He locked himself into that position for the rest of his life. He was willing to do this when it was necessary—but *only* when it was necessary.

And so it went throughout Coolidge's career. He avoided making enemies when there was no good reason to do so. In 1920, when he had his first shot at the presidency, his nomination was impeded by the powerful Senator Henry Cabot Lodge, and Coolidge ended up as vice president under Warren Harding instead. A less lucky man might have made a lifelong enemy out of Lodge by losing his cool and firing off a salvo of angry words. Coolidge did not, though many felt a few nasty remarks would have been justified under the circumstances. "Coolidge's secret thoughts of Lodge are not fit to print," former President Taft wrote. The point was that Coolidge did keep those thoughts secret, since there was no good reason to reveal them.

And since he did not utter the words that may have been in his mind, they did not come back to haunt him. In one of those unexpected twists of events that fill human life but that only the lucky are prepared for, Lodge found it expedient to support the idea of a Coolidge presidential candidacy in 1924. He could not easily have done so, and Coolidge could not easily have accepted the support, if they had been enemies. Both would then have been accused of shallow opportunism. As it was, Lodge was able to offer generous support, and he lived just long enough to learn of Coolidge's landslide victory in the 1924 election.

Calvin Coolidge was by all measures one of our luckiest presidents. He obviously knew a lot about luck—though just *what* he knew or thought, of course, nobody ever found out. Not only was he master of this Ninth Technique, but he seems also to have conquered the Fourth, the technique of run cutting. He cut his greatest run of luck short, and he did it brilliantly, just when the run was at its height, just when every loser in the world would have been gripped by greed and would have held on for more.

The four years of Coolidge's elected term, from early 1925 to early 1929, were years of absolutely unprecedented prosperity. The world had never seen anything like it. The "Coolidge prosperity," as it was universally called, was capitalism's finest hour to date. Americans themselves had trouble believing what was happening to them, and as for Europeans and Russians, they watched in pop-eyed amazement. Business boomed. Factory wages in America soared to more than twice what could be had anywhere in Europe and six times what could be earned in the workers' paradise, Russia. The stock market went wild. For every $100 you invested in General Motors common stock at its low in 1923, you found yourself sitting on $2,150 at the high in 1929. Thousands of ordinary middle-class citizens were getting rich.

It was a lovely time to be alive. And a fine time to be president. To have such a boom named after you—what more could a president ask for?

What more? Many presidents, probably most, would have said "four more years." Not Calvin Coolidge. This accomplished student of luck knew about run cutting.

One morning in August, 1927, he called some reporters to the White House and handed them each a slip of paper on which was a single astounding sentence: "I do not choose to run for president in 1928."

That was it. No elaborations. No explanations. Nothing but the plain, short statement: "I do not choose to run."

It was entirely in keeping with this inscrutable man's character that he had not discussed this decision with anybody, with the possible exception of one or two close friends. Many politicians and sundry autobiographers later came forward and said, "Oh, he'd told *me* months before." But one can doubt the truth of such claims. Coolidge's wife, Grace, was as startled by the announcement as anybody. Evidently he had never let slip, even to her, the faintest hint as to his thoughts about running in 1928.

He went home to his beloved New England. Unlucky Herbert Hoover succeeded him as president. A few months after Hoover took office, the great Coolidge run came to a disastrous end. The stock market crashed late in 1929. By the end of the following year, the nation and most of the world were in the grip of the worst depression in modern times.

Lucky Cal Coolidge, he was out of it. Was he content? Nobody knows. He never said.

IT IS A central assumption of modern psychology that talk is the cure for all ills and the route to all private and public heavens. Sigmund Freud was one who held this unlikely belief. He taught that if you are troubled, you can get cured by lying on your back, gibbering to a shrink. Neither he nor any of his disciples ever offered trustworthy evidence that this is true, but the idea caught the imagination of the Western world.

Today the volume of doctor-endorsed talk is vastly greater. Mass-media shrinks like Dr. Joyce Brothers assure us over and over again that "communication" is the key to marital bliss, sexual ecstasy, and whatever else one might want. In her books and magazine articles on these topics, Dr. Brothers has couples making lists. Lists of what they like and dislike. Lists of why they're mad, lists of why they're sad. And then they read these lists and they talk, talk, talk.

Part of the rationale is the century-old assumption that it is bad for you to "bottle up" your feelings. If you're angry, you are supposed to open the valves, let off the steam and reduce the pressure. Shrinks have been asserting this, without proving its correctness, ever since Freud's day and particularly in the very talky era that began in the 1960s. If you accept the analogy that men and women are vessels filled with steam under pressure, the assertion may make a goofy kind of sense. But the fact is that it is almost certainly untrue.

Studies at Cornell University and elsewhere have demonstrated, in fact, that the reverse is true. People who "bottle up" their anger—in other words, control it—don't come to any great harm. People who habitually vent their anger, on the other hand, only get angrier.

They get angrier largely because they continually stir up their environment. By lashing out at people, they provoke angry responses, to which they respond with still more anger. The let-off-steam kind of personality lives in a never-ending storm of blows and counterblows.

Calvin Coolidge, by contrast, habitually held his feelings in. If he felt anger—at somebody like Henry Cabot Lodge, for instance—he sat on it. A psychiatrist would almost certainly have advised Coolidge to let the anger out. But Coolidge knew better. He kept the lid on.

And where did it get him? The presidency.

It is unlikely that talk would have been of any more help in Coolidge's private life than in his public one. He and Grace were not in the habit of "communicating" a great deal, and the idea of making little lists would have amused them. Yet their marriage was so serene that it deeply moved Howard Chandler Christy, a painter who lived at the White House while working on the president's and the first lady's portraits.

Historians learned years later that silent Cal was not faithful to his wife. There is no conclusive evidence to tell us whether Grace knew about this and didn't care, knew about it and elected to ignore it, or didn't know about it. Perhaps she, too, sought sexual variety outside the marriage. Nobody knows for sure. What can be said for sure is that talk could not have improved the situation in the slightest and might have made it very much worse. It was a silent and uncommunicative marriage, but in its way, it worked. What would have been the sense of destroying it with talk?

SILENCE DOESN'T ONLY protect you from getting locked into unwanted positions, and it doesn't only keep you from revealing facts and feelings you may not want known. It has one other great virtue. By avoiding excessive communication, lucky men and women are freed of the need to explain and justify actions to other people.

Other people's opinions can tangle you and slow you disastrously. Typical sad story from Wall Street: The chronic loser buys some stock and blabs to his or her spouse, explaining all the reasons why this investment is so nifty. Bad luck obtrudes. The stock price plunges. This is the time when the speculator ought to apply the Fifth Technique, luck selection. The venture has soured, so it is time to discard bad luck before it becomes worse luck. It is time to sell out.

But the loser, being a loser, has communicated too much. Now the spouse is jeering. "You sure know how to pick them! Wow, what an expert! This nifty investment has cost us six thousand bucks so far. Boy, I hope it doesn't get any niftier!"

The jeering may not be so baldly spoken. It may be merely implied by looks or gestures. It may even be entirely unintended. It may be simply *felt* by the loser. No matter. There it is, and its effect is to jam the valuable Fifth Technique and make it unusable. The loser finds it impossible to say "I was wrong." Instead, he is forced to take a stand: "This is just temporary, I tell you! Just wait. I'll be proved right in the end!"

And down the drain go the talky two.

Since life is ruled by luck and you can never predict what actions you will need to take, it is best to say as little as possible about what you are doing and thinking. Then, when action is required, the only person you must argue with is yourself. That is often tough enough.

A New York psychiatrist—one of the few on earth who doesn't urge his patients to keep their mouths going all the time—tells of a woman who communicated too much to her son and daughter. She had absorbed the doctrine of nonstop communication when they were grade school kids in the 1960s. Everybody in the world seemed to think it was a good idea for parents to have frequent "frank talks" with kids. Teachers thought it, school shrinks thought it, magazine articles repeated it endlessly, and only the consistently lucky questioned it.

When the woman and the kids' father were divorced, she conducted the required frank talks with her kids about the episode. When she joined a local chapter of Parents Without Partners, a service and social organization of the widowed and divorced, she felt it incumbent upon her to explain her reasons to the youngsters. When she began meeting new men friends, she told the kids much more than they needed to know and probably a good deal more than they wanted to know. They may have wished their mother would shut up and leave them alone. But she was only doing what every good parent was supposed to do.

The "frank talk" dogma was widely preached in Parents Without Partners' chapter newsletters and its national magazine, *The Single Parent,* during the 1960s and 1970s. But around 1980, many PWP members seem to have come to feel that the dogma was overrated. Some, indeed, arrived at the conclusion that it was plain rubbish. "What earthly good is it going to do to discuss my private life and feelings with my kids?" one woman wrote. "To the extent that my divorce directly affects their lives, they're entitled to hear from me. But as for *why* I got divorced, it's none of their business."

That determinedly silent woman may well have been a lucky one. But the woman who is the subject of this case story was too talky to be lucky.

Unlike many of her fellow PWP members, she continued the practice of nonstop communication in the 1980s. Her son and daughter were now adults. She continued to shower them with unsolicited details of her affairs with men.

There was one man in whom she invested more than a trivial amount of emotional capital. She met him at a PWP function. He was an early-retired teacher. He and she got into the habit of doing things as a couple. She then started inviting him to traditional family gatherings such as Christmas dinner. Finally, he suggested that their sexual and financial convenience could both be served by his moving into her apartment and sharing the rent.

She gave a detailed account of this progression to her son and daughter. It was a mistake, for in doing so she gave away her freedom to act in her own best interest.

The son found the retired teacher congenial enough, but the daughter took an immediate and instinctive dislike to the man. Certain clues made her suspect that he was in fairly desperate financial straits and had joined PWP at least partly with the purpose of finding somebody to support him.

"He's nothing but a charming golddigger," the daughter said. In time her brother came around to that view, too.

The mother earnestly denied it. "If he's after money," she pointed out, "there are lots of richer women around than me."

This was true. On the other hand, the mother did have a comfortable middle-class income and nest egg. This was more than the ex-teacher seemed to have.

Unwilling to let her son and daughter think she had any doubts about this man in whom she had invested so much, the mother went along with his suggestion and invited him to move in with her. She did it as much in a spirit of defiance as for any other reason. She was going to *show* her son and daughter that she had faith in her own judgment.

If she had kept her thoughts to herself all along, she would not have needed to show anybody anything. Her only debating opponent then would have been herself. But she had invited other people's opinions into her life. Those opinions had begun to push her in directions she might not have chosen if she had been free.

It got worse. By bad luck, the ex-teacher had a heart attack soon after moving in with her. It was not serious; he recovered fast. But it was expensive, and it worsened his already bad financial condition. He was unable to pay his share of the rent or even contribute much to the food budget.

The woman, through her job, was enrolled in a group health insurance program that would have paid for the man's illness had he been her spouse. It would not pay for a nonmarital partner, however. For this and other reasons, the ex-teacher began to talk about their getting married.

She was now beginning to feel some of the doubts expressed by her daughter. The man was charming, but was he just looking for a free ride? With these doubts mounting, she should have cut her losses, abandoned her investment, and withdrawn from the venture long ago. But she could not make herself say "I was wrong"—particularly to her son and daugh-

121

ter. She talked herself into hoping for the best and, then, into believing the best. She talked herself into optimism—a dangerous state of mind, as we've seen in other contexts. She married the man.

It turned out disastrously. The man was not only broke; he was up to his ears in debt. His creditors now began dunning his new spouse. The total of their demands was more than her life savings. The marriage disintegrated under the strain. Eventually the ex-teacher ran off with another woman, leaving his wife a good deal poorer and, perhaps, wiser.

If he left her less talky than he found her, then some good may have come out of the miserable situation. The psychiatrist who told me this story, counselor to many PWP members in the New York area, says that excessive talk seems to be a contributing factor to the troubles of many of those life-scarred people. He doesn't discuss the phenomenon in terms of luck. What he does say is that the talkiest marriages often seem to be the shortest lasting. "These 'frank' and 'open' kinds of relationships are volatile," he says. "They tend to blow up."

The reason is luck—the continual intrusion of the unexpected. Once you realize that luck is always going to play a dominant role in your life, you become aware that anything you say may turn against you. A statement that seems safe today may become dangerous in the changed circumstances of tomorrow. The friend to whom you whisper a confidence today may be your enemy tomorrow. If you talk too much about a venture this year, you may find you've given away your freedom when you want to get out of it next year.

It doesn't mean you must take a vow of eternal silence. You must have relationships, after all; you must take chances; you must talk to people. The message of the Ninth Technique is only that you avoid unnecessary talk about your problems, plans, and feelings. When there is no *good* reason to say something, say nothing.

# 12. The Tenth Technique: Recognizing a Nonlesson

There are experiences in life that seem to be lessons but aren't. A noteworthy trait of the lucky is that they know what they can't learn anything from.

"Twice in a row I had a hunch about a stock but didn't buy it, and the doggone stock doubled. I've sure learned my lesson! Next hunch I get, I'm going to back it with everything I've got!"

A good piece of learning? No, a potentially disastrous one. All the investor has really learned is that good and bad luck happen.

"I've been married twice, and my husbands both cheated me. I'll never trust a man again."

"I just realized: Every time I go to the track with Marie, I win. So from now on . . ."

"Seems like every time I quit my job, there's a shake-up and the person in the job gets promoted. Boy, have I learned my lesson! I'll stay in *this* job till I get what's coming to me."

Nonlessons, all of them. It goes back to the First Technique, learning how to make clear distinctions between luck and planning. When outcomes are brought about by random events that are not under anybody's control—events that we would define collectively as luck—then you must be very careful in determining what lessons may be drawn from them. The habit of deriving false lessons from life's random happenings is a trait of the unlucky.

Nonlessons often grow out of unwarranted generalizations. A certain kind of event happens a few times in association with a certain kind of person, and you make a sweeping generalization to include all people of that kind. Many feminists, for example, are women who, by bad luck, have had several unhappy experiences at the hands of men. The generalization: "All men are untrustworthy." Or "All men are rapists at heart." Similarly, many divorced men are bitter toward all of the opposite sex. "Never trust a woman. You give her half a chance, she'll steal everything you've got."

It is perfectly true that some men are rapists at heart and some women are larcenous. It may be your bad luck to encounter such an individual at some time in your life. It may even be your worse luck to have your life affected by more than one. But if that happens, it will be important not to derive a misleading lesson from the experience. Recognize that you have received a nonlesson. You have learned nothing except that bad luck happens.

Taking that kind of false lesson seriously may or may not do you grave harm. In the wrong circumstances, it can cripple you. If you withdraw from the fast flow because of a couple of unhappy experiences, you may achieve your purpose of shielding yourself against bad luck; but you also shield yourself against good luck.

Another kind of nonlesson, just as common but less obvious, comes from the belief that history is going to repeat itself. People who hold this belief believe, as a corollary, that you can learn detailed lessons for the future by studying the past.

All kinds of otherwise smart people subscribe to this peculiar dogma. They enjoy quoting pithy statements on the topic: "Those who persistently fail to learn the lessons of history are doomed to repeat it." This statement has been variously attributed to several nineteenth-century statesmen, who in turn may have plagiarized it from somebody still earlier. It's clever, but is it true? Unfortunately, no, except in the most vague and general way.

124

History simply does not repeat itself. Why should it? History is the product of what billions of men and women are doing, thinking, and feeling at a given time. It is in constant flux. It is entirely unpredictable. Lessons? As Henry Ford put it, "History is bunk."

Certainly it can teach huge, generalized lessons such as "War is hell." But can it teach us how to stay out of wars? Of course not. If it could, the world would be at peace. If it were possible to study history and say, "Oh yes, *that's* how to do it!" then the world's nations would have chosen peace long ago.

Unfortunately, history offers no such lessons. Every war starts because of a unique combination of mistakes, bad luck, bad responses, and other factors—a combination that is never repeated. Studying wars of the past is unlikely to be of the slightest help in preventing those that may face us in the future, including the big one that everybody has nightmares about.

And it is the same in your personal and financial life. Certainly, there are some lessons that can be derived from past experience—very useful lessons, at times. You can often judge an individual's future behavior, for instance, by consulting the record: How did he or she behave in similar situations in the past? This accumulation of knowledge about an individual is the basis of trust, without which human life could not work at all. The more "history" you collect on the men and women who play important roles in your life, the more you trust them (or don't trust them, as the case may be). These historical lessons about individuals aren't infallible, but they turn out right often enough to be a useful and ubiquitous part of our daily dealings with each other.

But beware history's nonlessons. A Merrill Lynch account executive tells of a customer who had what he thought was an infallible system for trading in gold. The customer had gone back through years of records and painstakingly compiled a detailed history of important ups and downs in the yellow metal's market price. He carefully noted what else was happening in the financial world at the times of gold's major price swings, and from this exhaustive history, he derived what he called "indicators" of price moves to come. Just before the market price of gold posted a major gain, he noted, the stock market was always in a slump, though utility stocks were up; bond yields were zigzagging in a certain pattern; residential housing sales were recovering from a dip; and so on. To make money in gold, he determined, all he had to do was wait until all or most of his indicators clicked into place, then buy.

The theory, of course, was that history was going to repeat itself.

"He had beautiful charts and tables," the Merrill Lynch man recalls wistfully. "It sure *looked* like it ought to work."

Unfortunately, it didn't work. You can often predict what one individual will do, but only in rare circumstances can you predict what a lot of people will do. The market price of gold, or any other fluid-priced speculative entity such as real estate or stocks, is the end product of millions of people's feelings, thoughts, and actions, all churning together and reacting one against another. The factors determining that end product, the price on a given day, are so many and so staggeringly complex that they are entirely beyond anybody's ability to control or predict. The situation, in other words, is one in which the dominant influence is luck; and when any piece of history is influenced by luck to that extent, it cannot be expected to repeat itself reliably.

The man with the infallible gold trading system had not realized this. He had combed through history in the hopes of picking up useful lessons: "*This* and *this* and *this* are things that happen before the price of gold goes up."

What he got was a nonlesson. True, his indicators *had* preceded a gold price jump several times in the past. But why? No reason, just luck. Pure, random chance had made history repeat itself, or seem to. Was there a good reason to believe it would happen that way in the future? No, there was none.

The man bet a lot of money on some gold-mining stocks at what he judged was the right time. It turned out to be the wrong time. The stocks' prices sagged. He might have saved himself if he had been master of the Fifth Technique: luck selection. But he didn't have that technique to help him either. Several years later, he is still waiting to get his money back.

HOW CAN YOU tell whether a historical outcome was caused by luck or by something more reliable, such as a person's character? One good way is to ask whether there are clearly visible links of cause and effect.

In the case of a person's character, character itself is the linking mechanism. A situation is brought to bear on Mary Smith; she responds in a certain way because it is her nature to do so. When the same situation arises next week, you can reasonably expect history to repeat itself. Of course, you can be fooled. There is an element of luck in this, as in all human phenomena. Mary Smith's character may change in time, or she may act out of character for unknowable reasons on certain occasions, or your reading of her character may be flawed. Still, this element of luck is not large. If you make judgments and predictions based on Mary's character, your chances of being right are tolerably good.

But in the case of the infallible gold trading system, there were no clear links of cause and effect. The man merely observed that on a few occasions in the past, there seemed to be a relationship between certain events in the housing industry and the price of gold. But what was the relationship? What caused what, and how? He didn't know. And that should have warned him that he was about to lose money on a nonlesson.

You can watch people in gambling casinos studying similar nonlessons every night of the week. They will watch a certain slot machine or roulette wheel for weeks and weeks. Some even keep records in little notebooks. They then invent nonlessons by which to guide their play. Some of these nonlessons are highly complicated, while others are the soul of simplicity. A roulette watcher might note, for example, that whenever the wheel turns up a number containing the digit 6, the number 28 comes up within the next few coups. "Aha!" the watcher says, convinced that he has discovered a Great Truth, hidden from everyone else. Now all he has to do, he believes, is wait until another 6 turns up and put his money on 28. And the house collects another sucker's money to sweeten its earnings report.

The watcher's calculations were based on a piece of history generated entirely by luck. The convergence of 6 and 28 a few times was random and accidental. That kind of history simply cannot be counted on to repeat itself. If it does happen to repeat itself, the recurrence will be nothing more than the extension of a run of luck. But as we saw in our studies of the Fourth Technique, runs are much more likely to be short than long.

I have been playing 6 and 28 on roulette wheels and in lotteries for many years; but I do it strictly in accordance with the Seventh Technique; constructive supernaturalism. As I mentioned earlier I regard them as my lucky numbers because they represent my birthday, June 28. They are also the only two "perfect" numbers on a roulette wheel—indeed, the only perfect whole numbers below 100.

That makes them perfectly lovely numbers. My attention is always drawn to them, even in situations in which I am not a participant. When I see them involved in apparent runs of luck, I feel a strong temptation to concoct nonlessons. "Those two numbers are *always* in the money!" It is a temptation that must be steadfastly resisted.

Several years ago, while in New Jersey on a business trip, I learned from a newspaper that the winning number in the previous day's "Pick-It" lottery was 628. This didn't do anything for me financially, since I wasn't in the game, but it did give me a happy little buzz. A couple of weeks later, back home in Connecticut, I was astonished to read that 286 had turned up as the winner in the state's daily lottery.

Was Lady Luck trying to send me some kind of signal? It was tempting to think so. The temptation became almost overwhelming when I picked up my morning newspaper a day later, turned to the financial pages, and studied the previous day's action on the New York Stock Exchange. There was a certain stock that I had been watching for several months. I had thought of buying it, had finally determined that the odds of success weren't attractive enough, but still couldn't get it out of my mind. When I checked the stock that day, the first number that hit me in the eye was the day's trading volume: 628 round lots.

What a temptation! Those lucky numbers of mine had been winners twice in recent history while I was watching. Could it happen a third time? Would the run continue?

I took myself firmly in hand and said, *no.* If one would be lucky, one must know what one can't learn anything from. The recent history of those numbers offered no lessons about the future. I refrained from buying any of the stock.

That was a lucky piece of inaction. Not more than a few weeks later, the trading price plunged on bad earnings news and stayed down for several years.

# 13. The Eleventh Technique: Accepting an Unfair Universe

Rabbi Harold Kushner believed he had always led an essentially blameless life. Being human he had undoubtedly broken some of God's laws and man's, but not many and not big ones. He thought he was, in general, a good man. He was demonstrably holier than most. Despite his human flaws and transgressions, he certainly did not deserve any terrible punishment.

But terrible punishment is what he got. Worse, the punishment was not inflicted on him directly but on his son, Aaron, an innocent child.

When Aaron was three, doctors determined that he was afflicted with a disease called progeria, or rapid aging. The horrified rabbi and his wife were told that there was no known cure. Their little boy would probably never grow much beyond three feet in height, would have no hair, would develop a wizened, aged appearance while still a child, and would probably not live beyond his early teens. The elements of this discouraging prognosis all happened as expected, and the boy died at the age of fourteen.

Filled with grief and rage. Rabbi Kushner asked: *Why?* Why was this done to him and his family? Why to a child? Why at all?

Seeking a plausible and acceptable answer, he embarked on a long, difficult intellectual journey. He described this journey in the 1981 book *When Bad Things Happen to Good People.*

At the end of the journey, he found that the answer he sought was the simplest of all possible answers, yet the hardest for a religious man to believe. It was this: The affliction of his son happened for no reason at all. It was just a random stroke of bad luck. Bad luck is just—well, bad luck.

It was not the answer most clergy people are taught, nor the one they lay on their flocks. Nor was it the answer asserted in the Bible.

THE BIBLE SAYS not once but many times that God runs a fair world. "Consider, what innocent ever perished, or where have the righteous been destroyed?" asks the Book of Job. And in Proverbs it says, "No ills befall the righteous, but the wicked are filled with trouble."

Unfortunately, it simply isn't true. There is a lot of wishful thinking in the Bible, and this is a particularly stark example of it. Ills *do* befall the righteous, and conversely, the wicked are often allowed to live happily ever after. All of us, the good, the bad, and the in-between, are equally likely to realize our fondest dreams or contract cancer.

It is essential that you grasp this truth, for failure to do so is a leading cause of bad luck. We will see why later. For now, just fix the fact firmly in your mind. *The fact is that fairness is a human concept. The rest of the universe knows nothing of it.*

It took Rabbi Kushner a long time to arrive at this conclusion. Along the way, he had to consider and reject a dozen or more religious explanations of bad luck—which, since they had been his gospel, he had always assumed to be the truth. All of us get these explanations handed to us as kids, and nearly all believe them for a time in our young lives; but the consistently lucky eventually tend to reject them as the rabbi did.

They really do not make a great deal of sense. The three most common religious explanations—so common that they amount to clerical clichés—are that God sends us bad luck to punish us for our sins, to teach us moral lessons, or to strengthen our characters.

All these explanations are intended, in Rabbi Kushner's words, to "defend God's honor." They are meant to convince the skeptical that God is really fair after all. The only reason why he *seems* unfair, we're told, is that we are too dumb to understand his great plans and purposes.

But one can ask why a three-year-old child needs to be punished with a fatal disease. If the little boy was guilty of a sin of some kind, wouldn't a slap on the wrist have been enough? Or if the father was the one being punished, and if his sin was bad enough to warrant a sentence of death, why was the sentence carried out on the youngster? In any case, why was no explanation ever offered as to the nature of the supposed sin? How can it teach a moral lesson to punish somebody without saying what lesson is supposed to be learned? Any sensible parent knows that if you are going to spank a child, you should make sure the child knows what it's for. Is God less sensible or less fair? One can ask, too, how it can have strengthened Aaron's character to kill him.

Millions of words of religious sophistry have been read from the world's pulpits in answer to such questions. Ministers, priests, and rabbis all react to the questions in the same way: "God is *too* fair! You just don't understand God's reasons!"

Rabbi Kushner, as we've seen, arrived at a simpler and almost certainly truer explanation—truer because it is supported by the plainly observable facts of human life. In the rabbi's theology, God may be fair but isn't as powerful as everybody has always thought. He either can't or won't control all the details of what happens to us. Our lives are filled with random events. If you contract a fatal disease or win a million-dollar lottery prize, therefore, don't look for the hand of God in the event. God didn't cause it. Nothing caused it. It just happened.

Rabbi Kushner thinks God may still be in the process of creating order from chaos. In the six days of creation, it's still Friday afternoon. God may get the universe straightened out a few billion years from now, and then life will be orderly and fair. Meantime, we've got to deal with what we see around us today, and that is chaos.

You don't have to buy the rabbi's theology if you don't want to. It is essentially irrelevant to our study of luck. The observable facts of human life can be explained just as well by postulating that God is out to lunch, is dead, or never existed in the first place. Or invent your own theology. It doesn't matter what it is, as long as you feel comfortable with it and as long as it doesn't try to argue away the facts.

For no matter how earnestly we talk, the facts won't change. The universe isn't fair and never has been in all the time men and women have been grappling with it. By accepting that truth instead of arguing with it, you take one more step on the road to becoming consistently lucky. Conversely, by arguing with it, you buy bad luck.

One way in which unlucky people commonly do this is to punish themselves for their own bad luck, thus, making it into worse luck. They get themselves stuck on a down-spiraling slide, sometimes stuck for life. I learned of an unusually stark example of this syndrome while studying some life-story material dealing with my college classmates.

I went to Princeton University right after the Second World War and graduated with the class of 1949. The Forty-niners, as we call ourselves, are all men, since Princeton did not start admitting women as undergraduates until exactly twenty years after we graduated. We are today in our late fifties or early sixties, looking back on nearly four decades of adult life.

Being a somewhat introspective group, we poll ourselves from time to time in order to find out how we've been doing and what we've been thinking. As one of the class scribes and as a student of luck, I have written up the results of these polls and have also interviewed individual class members and their wives. My files on these polls and interviews are a fascinating collection of lessons on getting lucky.

The 750-plus members of the class have of course had widely diverse life experiences since we left the campus with our diplomas clutched in our young hands. Some have risen to national prominence: for example, Federal Reserve chairman, Paul Volcker; and one-time New Jersey governor, Brendan Byrne. Others—myself, for one—have enjoyed good fortune without any accompanying fame. But a probably equal number of other Forty-niners have been hit by bad luck in one form or another. Somewhat more than one hundred have suffered the ultimate misfortune of a too-early death in war, by accident, and by disease.

It is one of the latter who is the subject of the story I want to tell. This man and his wife—we'll call them John and Mary—were married in a Catholic church early in the 1950s. They were not particularly observant Catholics back then. Though they had no doubts about their religious orientation—if you asked them what church they belonged to, they would reply "Catholic" without hesitation—they were fairly casual in their approach to church rituals and forms. They sometimes skipped the Sunday morning service if they had been up late at a party the night before, and they didn't participate conscientiously in sacramental acts such as Holy Communion. This troubled Mary a good deal more than John. She would remark often that they were losing something good from their lives because of sheer laziness. He would agree, then shrug, and the following Sunday they would skip the Mass again.

Despite this slow loss of religious commitment, both of them clung firmly to the belief that God runs a fair universe. This is an element of religious teaching that every Catholic child learns from priests and nuns in catechism classes. Whatever happens in human life is God's will. If you want good luck in a certain chancy situation, you say a prayer; and if God decides you deserve to be rewarded, you will be. If you get walloped by bad luck, on the other hand, that is God's hand at work, too. You are being tested, or are getting your character strengthened, or are being punished.

John and Mary had a daughter whom they loved. When she announced that she found catechism boring, they didn't force her to attend. They knew from their own experience that religious instruction, inspiring when well taught, can be stupefyingly dull to a child when taught by rote—and this is particularly true of Catholic instruction. And so John's and Mary's daughter grew up as a nominal Catholic but not an actively participating one.

Shortly after her eighth birthday, on the very day when she would have received her First Holy Communion if she had followed the normal schedule, she was abducted, raped, and killed.

It was a case of particularly ghastly bad luck—random evil reaching out and seizing an innocent victim for no reason except that she was there. John and Mary, however, could not accept a universe so unfair. In the theology that had been pounded into them since childhood, God was everywhere. Holding this view, they saw their daughter's horrible death as their fault. God had caused it to punish them for their impiety.

Bad luck is hard enough to take when you recognize it as bad luck. When you blame yourself for it, it can destroy you.

John, the least pious of the pair before the tragedy, reacted the most strongly. He became so grimly devout that Mary found herself trying to pull him in the opposite direction. "I got over the guilt thing after a while, or almost did," she told me later, "but with him it was an obsession. I tried to get him to talk to a psychiatrist about it, but he wouldn't. He did talk to a priest, but the priest wasn't any help."

John grew moody and depressed. Bad luck was turning to worse luck. In time, it became still worse. His career as a bank executive started to suffer as colleagues and customers noticed the souring of his disposition. He became irritable, uncooperative, sometimes rude. Then a new stroke of bad luck came crashing into his life. Through a chain of events that he had no hand in, the bank got itself tangled up in a scandal involving illegal foreign-currency operations. The affair was not only embarrassing to the bank but also fearfully costly. It was necessary to find somebody to blame, and John was it. He had angered many of his fellow executives in recent months, so they found it easy to make him the target. They all scurried for cover, leaving him exposed. He lost his job.

Once again he analyzed the situation in terms of a fair universe. There had to be a *reason* for this new disaster, he believed. What could the reason be? Obviously, God was punishing him again.

If you lose your job because of events that are not of your making, the unhappy episode may knock you down but needn't knock you out. It needn't, that is, as long as you see clearly that what has happened to you is only a case of bad luck. But if you automatically assume that every bad thing that happens to you is in some way your own fault, then, bad luck will almost always become worse luck.

Discouraged and hopeless, John slunk home to sit in an armchair and watch TV for the rest of his life. Mary could not get him out of that chair. He was convinced, she believes, that he deserved what had happened to him. It was God's will, so why fight it? He ate, drank, and smoked too much and was dead of a heart attack before age sixty.

Rabbi Kushner tells a similar story of a Jewish couple who, hit by misfortune, concluded that they were being punished for a too-casual approach to religious observances. "Religion made them feel worse," he notes sadly.

Does the rabbi counsel you, therefore, to shun religion? Of course not. He says only that you should recognize chaos when you see it. Chaos is not dangerous until it begins to look orderly. That is the lesson of this Eleventh Technique. Look around at human life and accept it the way it comes: disorderly and unfair. Don't shun religion if it appeals to you. Shun only the ancient belief that God plans and directs every event in your life.

JUST AS IT is misleading to blame yourself for bad luck, you also delude yourself when you come to a belief that you "deserve" good luck. You may well deserve it, but whether you will get it is a matter of—well, luck.

Shakespeare's difficult but powerful play *King Lear* has offended many critics, including Charles Lamb, mainly because it is the story of a lot of people who deserve good luck but don't get it. As we've noted before in this book, literary critics and college English professors hate to acknowledge the role of luck in novels and dramas. In their view, bad luck isn't "tragic" enough. They prefer stories in which heroes and heroines bring about their own doom through their own wickedness or foolishness. However, such an orderly arrangement of events bears scant relationship to real life. In real life, people don't get what they deserve. They get what they get.

Shakespeare evidently understood this. The unfortunate Lear, and his loving daughter Cordelia, and his loyal follower Gloucester are all good people who deserve good luck. What do they get? Gloucester is blinded, Cordelia is killed, and Lear goes mad and finally dies of grief. What is this supposed to teach us? Generations of English professors have tried to convince skeptical students that Lear and the others are brought to these bad ends by "fatal flaws" in their own characters. However, these fatal flaws are mainly in the professors' imaginations; they aren't in the play. In the play as written, the main cause of the characters' doom is sheer bad luck.

Never go into a venture thinking it will come out right for you because you "deserve" it. That is a common expectation of the unlucky. The universe has no interest in what you deserve.

Nor is the universe interested in the "my turn" expectation, also common among the unlucky. This, too, comes from the assumption that the universe is fair.

"All my college friends have lucked into super jobs. I'm the only one of our group left out in the cold. My turn must be coming soon!"

"My first two marriages were nightmares. Surely I've had my share of misfortune. The third time has got to be better."

Such expectations might be reasonable if the sharing out of good and bad luck were under human control. Humans would make a mind-numbing bureaucracy out of the Luck Administration but would instinctively try to run it fairly. That is the way humans are. Our sense of fairness is powerful. The universe, however, is not under human control. It is indifferent to the concept of fairness, which we prize so highly, and so it is always confounding and enraging us.

Go to a casino any day or night, and you will see the pockets of unlucky gamblers being inexorably emptied by the expectation of fairness. If a roulette wheel turns up odd numbers three or four times in a row, at least half the players are likely to think some kind of "debt" is building up. The wheel supposedly "owes" it to the cause of fairness to produce an even number next time around.

Unfortunately, the wheel doesn't know this. It has no memory and would have no interest in fairness even if it did keep score. The probability of an even number next time around is exactly the same as it always was: fifty-fifty.

This paradox of unfairness confuses a lot of people. In any situation such as the repeated spinning of a roulette wheel, fairness seems to crop up over a long period of time. If you spin the wheel a thousand times, you can expect that odd and even numbers will turn up roughly five hundred times each. That seems fair. It is the same with any other series of events in which there are two or more equally likely outcomes: tossing a coin, for instance, or rolling a die. If the die is properly balanced and if you roll it six thousand times, the six sides will turn up very roughly one thousand times each.

But if you try to work this apparent fairness into a system for betting on individual rolls of the die, you are setting yourself up for a loss. The rolls are unrelated to each other. Each is a separate event. It is not influenced in the slightest by rolls that preceded it, and it will have no effect on rolls that follow.

This is an outrage to our human sense of fairness. It is always tripping crapshooters. They will note that no sixes have turned up on either of a pair of dice during a long period of play. The dice, therefore, are said to be "six heavy." Some cosmic force is supposedly building up a six-weighted tension in the dice, and this tension will get stronger and stronger until the dice pay off their debt. Many players will adjust their betting accordingly.

The idea is entirely fallacious. Like the roulette wheel, the dice have neither a memory nor a sense of fairness.

Bridge players delude themselves in the same way. "The last two times I tried to finesse, the card that killed me was to my left. This time, it's bound to be to my right."

As we saw in our study of the Seventh Technique, constructive supernaturalism, this kind of semisuperstitious thinking can be useful sometimes. In a situation in which there is no rational basis for making a choice, it can save you from paralysis. When you've got to do *something*, it can help you reach a decision—but be sure you know precisely what you are doing and why. Maintain a keen awareness that you are resorting to a supernatural device because it is the only way out. Never fall back on the supernatural in the belief that it is science or will give you a palpable advantage. And never use it when a rational analysis would serve instead.

In the game of bridge, there are various kinds of rational clues that can be used to pinpoint the location of a feared card. These clues pop up in both the bidding and the play. They may not make you perfectly certain who is holding the queen of spades, but they can lead you to a solid, analytic conclusion: "Odds are it's to my left."

Never fall back on the supernatural when this kind of analysis is possible. Only when there are no clues at all or when clues of equal weight seem to point in opposite directions, should you trust your fate to any irrational decision-making process such as a notion about fairness.

"Never *expect* anything," said one of the luckier Forty-niners, Alvaro Cruz. "Anything can happen no matter how outrageous it seems. And anything can *not* happen no matter how much you think it should."

Cruz was talking about a friend of his and mine, Bob Baumer. Bob had served with the Fifteenth Air Force in Europe during World War II and had been shot down twice, narrowly escaping with his life each time. "There were guys who flew more missions than I did and never got touched," he used to say. "If I ever fly in a war again, fate won't *dare* do it to me a third time."

Bob went back into the air force during the Korean War. On June 10, 1952, the unfair universe did it to him again. His B-29 was shot down while on a bombing mission, and he was killed.

# 14. The Twelfth Technique: The Juggling Act

Think of some lucky people you know, and then think of some you consider unlucky. One highly visible difference is almost sure to stand out: The luckier are the busier.

Lucky people always seem to have many ventures going on at the same time. Even at the height of success in a major venture such as a career, the lucky man or woman will usually have secondary ventures going or in preparation or under study—sometimes in bewildering variety. This affords protection in case the major venture runs into bad luck—which can happen unexpectedly at any time, as no lucky person ever forgets. If Venture A turns sour or simply turns stagnant and unexciting, maybe Venture B or C will burst into flames in some unexpected way.

But if the lucky individual seems busy when things are going well, you will find him or her still busier in adversity. Yes, the lucky have their ups and downs like anybody else. The difference is that, with the lucky, down periods never last long and often end in surprising, unforeseen ways. Consider the delightful story of Charles Darrow.

Darrow's story is one of the classic legends of luck. His brainchild is known throughout the world, but his own name is familiar only to a few. They talk of him fondly and reverently as the Man Who Passed "Go."

Darrow was a forty-two-year-old heating engineer living in Germantown, Pennsylvania, in 1933. He was basically a lucky man, but now he was involved in an episode of worldwide bad luck, the Great Depression. He had not had a steady job for three years.

As is typical of the lucky, however, he had a whole conglomeration of ventures going. He continued to seek work in his main profession as a heating engineer, but that didn't keep him nearly busy enough. He established an appliance-repair business, which did fairly well in a time when people couldn't afford new appliances. He also set himself up as an expert in repairing cracked concrete walls and walks. This business, too, made sense in a cost-conscious time. Thinking his way along a completely different track, Darrow also wondered about starting a low-cost boarding kennel and veterinary service. He began by visiting a local vet and arranging to work as a dog walker in exchange for instruction.

All this was a typically lucky reaction to adversity. The unlucky personality would seek just one way out of a hole—the obvious way: "I gotta find another job!" But Darrow's reaction was more likely to bring success. His thinking went something like this: "It would be nice to find another job. I'll try. But in case I don't run into good luck along that route, I'd better look for luck in some other directions at the same time."

The unlucky person knows exactly what form of luck he is seeking. If he does get lucky, the good luck will come in one shape only: a new job. Charles Darrow, by contrast, didn't know just what he was hoping for. All he knew was that the more ventures he got himself into, the better were the odds that some kind of lucky break would come his way.

As it turned out, the big break that came crashing into his life, turning it upside down, was of a nature that startled even him.

Like millions of other middle-income Americans in the balmy 1920s, Darrow had been a small-time plunger in the stock market. Now, in the bleak winter of 1933, he dreamed of how nice it would be to be rich. He reviewed his penny-ante Wall Street successes and failures in his mind. What would have become of him if he had done *this* instead of *that?* Suppose he had sold his General Motors stock when it was trading above one thousand dollars a share instead of waiting till it crashed to forty dollars? What would he do with that hypothetical money if he had it today? Put it into real estate, perhaps. People were making killings on land and buildings even during the depression. Darrow and his wife entertained themselves at meals by talking of ways in which they could become real-estate tycoons.

It then occurred to Darrow that this kind of game might be absorbing to other people. Perhaps, he thought, depression-weary people would find it fun to play a game in which they could imagine themselves playing with big money.

Darrow was handy with tools. Occasionally, he had made jigsaw puzzles and other games for fun. Now, he found a large, round piece of oilcloth and sketched a schematic design of streets and housing plots on it. He gave the streets real names from Atlantic City, where he had enjoyed vacations in more prosperous times. Then, he colored the design with free paint samples from a local store. Next, he scrounged some free scraps of wooden molding from a lumberyard, and he cut the scraps into small shapes resembling houses. He made title deeds from scraps of cardboard.

At first, he had only a vague idea of the rules under which the game should be played, but his thoughts grew more distinct as time went on. Using a pair of dice, some play money borrowed from a youngster, and colored buttons for tokens, Darrow and his wife and friends spent evenings and weekends playing the game. They refined it as they went along: added new rules, introduced new complications. As it finally evolved, the game had some kind of magic. People who were newly introduced to it would rapidly become fascinated and would want to go on playing all night.

Darrow called it Monopoly.

He saw it as a distinctly secondary venture in the beginning. Friends and neighbors asked him to make sets for them. He did, charging about a dollar a set. He was able to turn out two handmade sets a day, which was roughly the level of demand. The game was advertised solely through acquaintanceship networks. Somebody would buy a set and invite friends to play, and the friends would then ask Darrow to make a set for them. He sold about one hundred sets in this way. He was content with the slow trickle of orders. It never occurred to him that Monopoly might be anything more than a minor hometown industry. But then luck came blundering into the picture, with explosive results.

The first stroke of luck happened when Monopoly was introduced to a man who owned a small printing shop. It came about by sheer chance. The printer was visiting a friend. The friend had borrowed a Monopoly set for a game the previous night, and the set was still lying about on a table in the parlor. Because of that minor failure of housekeeping—the failure to pack away the set the night before—the history of Monopoly and the life of Charles Darrow were drastically altered. The printer looked at the game, was intrigued, and got himself invited back to play. After playing one game, he was hooked. A game so addictive, he thought, could be sold to a lot of people.

He approached Darrow and offered to print the Monopoly boards, fake money, and other paraphernalia. Darrow was delighted to be rid of the chore. The printer also launched a modest advertising and promotional campaign. He and Darrow upped production to six sets a day.

Then another stroke of luck added fuel to the developing fire. An official of a Philadelphia department store, motoring in the suburbs, developed engine trouble and pulled into a service station to get it fixed. While waiting, he strolled around the Main Street district of the town in which he happened to find himself. In a drug or variety store, he saw some Monopoly sets, placed there on consignment by the printer-promoter. The Philadelphia man liked the look and idea of the game instantly. He bought a set and took it home with him. A short time later, Darrow and the printer received an order for a wholesale lot of sets.

Monopoly was only a few months old, but Darrow suddenly found it growing beyond control. The Philadelphia store sold out its first shipment of sets and immediately ordered more. Word of the hot new game spread to other big Philadelphia stores, then to other cities. The stores began ordering in enormous quantities: one hundred sets at a time, 200, 300. The stores couldn't get them fast enough to satisfy the ever-growing demand. The printer couldn't make them fast enough, and Darrow was drowning in paper from the shipping, billing, and purchasing side of the business. He and the printer had created a monster that threatened to eat them alive.

There was only one way out. Darrow went to see Parker Brothers.

Parker Brothers, established in 1883 in Salem, Massachusetts, was the nation's biggest producer of table games. Darrow's idea was to license Monopoly to this big company on some kind of royalty basis.

Parker Brothers studied the game. The company had operated profitably for many years by sticking with some basic rules about what does and doesn't make a good table game. One rule was that a game should be simple. Another was that it should not take more than forty-five minutes to play out to a conclusion. Monopoly violated both these rules. It also violated others. All told, in Parker's analysis, the new game contained fifty-two "fundamental errors." The company turned Darrow down.

Back home in Pennsylvania, meanwhile, the Monopoly boom was still growing. Christmas, 1934, was approaching, and the stores were clamoring for more sets and still more. Darrow was exhausted and wanted to slow down, but the monster would not let him rest. He ordered a batch of five thousand new sets to be manufactured. All were sold to stores before they came off the printer's assembly line, while new orders poured in for thousands more.

Word of all this frantic activity got back to Parker Brothers. "Suddenly," a company report on the affair states, "fifty-two fundamental errors didn't seem so bad." Bravely admitting its mistake, Parker Brothers went back to Darrow, hat in hand, and offered him the royalty contract he had been seeking.

Darrow accepted, signed the contract and staggered off on vacation, so tired that it may have taken him a few days to realize how lucky he was. He was only in his early forties, but he would never need to work again for the rest of his life. A year back, he had been an unemployment statistic; now, he was rich and fast getting richer. A once-minor venture had propelled him to instant success.

I once asked Parker Brothers' president, Edward P. Parker, how much money Darrow earned all told from his fabulous venture; but Parker said that information was "of a confidential nature." He did allow, however, that Monopoly was by all measures the most successful product the company ever put on the market. It is produced in fifteen different languages. Some seventy-five million sets have been sold since Darrow signed that royalty contract. To supply all those sets with money, Parker Brothers has printed more than $1,000,000,000,000. That is a trillion dollars.

Lucky Charles Darrow was a millionaire many times over when he died in 1970, just short of his eightieth birthday. A lucky man indeed. But he was lucky because he put himself in position to be.

YOU NEVER KNOW what seemingly unpromising activity is going to be the one that catches fire for you. All you can know is that the more activities you have going on, the greater is the likelihood that *something* good will happen.

Charles Darrow certainly would not have guessed, back in 1933, that his big break would come from Monopoly. He might have thought some other venture looked more likely to succeed—the appliance-repair business, perhaps. But a table game? It didn't seem to be anything more than a sideline venture—a way to pick up a little spending cash while having fun. Who would have thought that would be the big one?

But that is the way luck operates. By its very nature, it isn't amenable to prediction. You cannot guess in advance what shape it will take or in what quarters it will strike. All you can do is what Darrow did: Cast out as many lines as possible to catch it.

Howard Hughes was a man who did that on a grander scale. It seems to have been a deliberate luck-changing effort on his part. He started out as nobody and ended as one of the richest people on earth, and he did it by juggling many ventures simultaneously.

In school, young Hughes's classmates thought of him as a born loser. He was one of those silent, ghostly youngsters who drift about on the fringes of schoolchild society. They come to school, they do their drab work, they go home. They leave no tracks. Years later, they vanish from memory. "No, I don't remember him at all. Are you sure he was in our class?"

But some kind of fire was ignited in Howard Hughes very suddenly after he left high school. Dozens of biographers and reporters have tried to find the source of that fire, without success. Hughes himself never offered any enlightenment. Teachers and classmates were at a loss to explain the change in their resident loser. But the explanation may really be quite simple. Hughes may have decided he wanted a luckier life. He was fed up with being a loser and wanted a new start. It happens that way often. People change because they decide they want to. No special trigger or traumatic event has to happen.

It is a common misconception that Howard Hughes inherited enormous wealth from his father. Not so. The senior Hughes left an estate valued at about six hundred thousand, which the eighteen-year-old Howard had to share with relatives. The main component of the estate was the Hughes Tool Company, maker of oil-field equipment. Three-quarters of the company's stock went to young Howard Hughes.

At that point in his life, he was no different from hundreds of other Texas kids whose parents had made money on oil. Most of those kids went nowhere. Their names ring no bells today. But young Howard Hughes was about to improve his luck. He saw his father's modest capital not as a cushion on which to sit and grow fat but as a bag of seeds that could be made to grow—provided somebody stood up, went out into the world, and sowed them.

The loser abruptly became a winner. Normally, when a minor inherits a controlling block of capital stock in a company, the stock is turned over to some kind of voting trust or other legal proxy until the youngster reaches twenty-one years of age. But young Hughes had suddenly become impatient to get going. To everybody's surprise, he went to court and argued that he was competent to vote the shares himself. Under Texas law, a judge could grant that wish if the youngster made a good case. Hughes did.

The Hughes Tool Company at the time was a very small, modestly prosperous company with a promising but by no means guaranteed future. Like Charles Darrow, who refused to pin his hopes solely on the chance of finding a new engineering job, young Howard Hughes decided that he needed other ventures besides the Hughes Tool Company. He plunged into a bewildering variety of them: movies, aircraft manufacturing, electronics, hotels and casinos, real estate, an airline. Not all of these ventures succeeded. His aircraft company, for instance, was never able to produce a salable military plane or an economically viable passenger carrier. But because he had other ventures going, good luck was likely to strike somewhere, and it did.

He made movies that are generally felt to be of mediocre artistic merit, but some of them, by luck, made a good deal of money. Quite by accident—by sheer, blind good luck—he made a stupendous amount of money on TWA stock. And so it went. His wealth when he died was estimated at more than a billion dollars.

What would have happened if, instead, he had pinned all his hopes on the Hughes Tool Company? There were times in its life when this company might have foundered but for infusions of money from other Hughes ventures. Without those other ventures, Howard Hughes could have died broke and unknown.

THIS TWELFTH TECHNIQUE is closely allied with the Second: fast-flow orientation; and the Sixth: the zigzag path. Taken together, they can keep you busy.

Busier than you think you want to be, perhaps. The lucky life is indeed characterized by a degree of hustle and bustle that seems frantic at times, especially to the chronically unlucky. As a candidate for good luck you will find yourself juggling many ventures that compete for your time and attention. Your life will be a whirl of people as you seek the fast flow. Instead of plodding toward a distant goal in a straight line, you will often be distracted by unexpected new opportunities that pop up to your left and right, and each one will require new decisions and more actions.

"She really is too busy," Elizabeth Arden's second husband said of her.

"She makes me dizzy." This man, a Russian expatriate named Prince Michael Evlanoff, seems to have led a generally luckless life until he married the cosmetics queen, but even that good luck did not last long. After two years, they couldn't stand each other and were divorced. Like many lucky people, Elizabeth Arden impressed some who knew her as being too busy for her own good—and she was certainly too busy to suit those who hoped to monopolize her time.

We've looked at her life in another context. It was the willingness to be busy that was the chief contributor to her lifelong good luck. After zigzagging through a number of possible careers, she started her first venture: a chain of beauty salons. But even that wasn't enough to guarantee lasting luck. The salons started brightly but eventually turned into money losers. Elizabeth Arden was saved by the fact that she had many other ventures going by the time the salon business turned sour.

She herself does not seem to have been troubled by the demands of a busy life. This is typical of the lucky. "I think I must look more harried than I feel," Senator Paula Hawkins of Florida said once to a group of reporters. Somebody had asked her if the typical Washington life of "rushing around" didn't take more out of her than it was worth. "I like 'rushing around,' as you call it," she said. "It isn't a life that was forced on me, it's a life I chose. I wouldn't be happy with a slower pace."

Senator Hawkins hit the nail on the head. The lucky life tends to look considerably more harried to others than it feels to the man or woman living it. Don't shy away from it out of fear that it will give you ulcers and high blood pressure. "It's a common item of pop psychology that being busy is bad for you," says University of Chicago psychologist Dr. Gene Gendlin. "There's no scientific basis for that belief. What counts is how you *feel* about being busy. If it feels good in the body, if it feels right, then for you it *is* right."

Dr. Gendlin is the author of a widely acclaimed book entitled *Focusing* in which he explains his method of zeroing in on what he calls the "bodily felt sense" of a problem or cluster of problems. Many people, he says, have such a big and busy array of worries that the very variety of them makes it hard to concentrate on any one and get it solved. In many cases these are potentially lucky people who have temporarily let themselves be overwhelmed by a busy life.

Dr. Gendlin suggests a simple and remarkably effective way out of this pickle: Sit down quietly and make a list of what your major worries are. It can be done mentally or in writing, as you prefer. Make no attempt to solve the problems. Simply acknowledge that they are there and stack them up in a pile, as it were. "Yes, there's that problem about my relationship with George, and there's that old one about my career, and there's the stock market making me nervous again."

The effect is exactly like that of making a things-to-do list before going away on vacation. Everybody is familiar with the kind of panic that can arise before you leave. In the last few days, you find yourself running around in circles. Every time you take care of one last-minute detail, you think of two more that need your attention. You run faster and faster and get dizzier and dizzier.

In that state, you are likely to do the very thing you fear: forget something important. How can you calm yourself? By sitting down and making a list of what needs to be done.

The list by itself doesn't get the jobs done, of course. What it does do is make you feel better. It gives you the sense of having regained control over a situation that was going haywire. In this more tranquil state, you can approach the indicated chores in a confident, orderly way.

Making a list of problems and worries produces the same state of calm, the feeling of control. Many people feel an actual, physical easing of tension in the body when they take this simple step. The easing is immediate and profound. Unlike a tranquilizing drug, this medicine can be taken as often as you wish.

Make a list of worries whenever your life seems to get too busy and you feel the beginnings of panic. In nearly all cases, you will find, the panic hasn't arisen because you have taken on too much; it has arisen, rather, because you have allowed an array of worries to get disorderly and uncontrolled. Each seems twice as bad because you have a lot of others snapping at your heels simultaneously, and the total effect is a feeling of thrashing about amid mounting chaos. Making a list restores order.

The luckiest men and women always find some way of juggling many ventures and activities successfully. If you seek good luck, it is far better to be too busy than not busy enough.

# 15. The Thirteenth Technique: Destiny Pairing

William Procter and James Gamble were young immigrants who drifted to Cincinnati in the 1830s. Procter was English, Gamble Irish. Until they met, they went nowhere. They were just two faceless statistics in the growing industrial city's labor pool. Both had jobs, at which they worked without particular distinction.

Then they met, and their lives changed radically.

They met when they courted a pair of sisters. It came about by blind chance, as such meetings usually do. One weekend the two young men came calling at the same hour, and they were introduced to one another in the sisters' parlor. The two liked each other instantly. Perhaps each recognized in the other some trait or group of skills or strengths that he had often wished to find in himself. Each determined, at any rate, that he had met a missing piece in the jigsaw puzzle of his life. Neither had made much of himself alone, but together, they may have sensed, they had the potential to go far.

They were destiny partners.

In 1837 they put their savings and some borrowed money together to form a tiny wad of seed capital. It totaled $7,192.24. With this small investment they founded a soap and candle business called Procter and Gamble. Business journalists ever afterward would misspell that first name "Proctor," but that didn't matter much. The company founded by the two young brothers-in-law (yes, they married the sisters) was to become perhaps the most successful mass marketer of low-priced household and food products in the history of the industrial world.

Throughout the 1980s, this enormous company has had more than $10 *billion* in sales each year. That is more than the gross national product of most of the world's countries—including Ireland, the native land of James Gamble.

That is what can happen when two people get together to expand their individual destinies. Apart: two also-rans. Together: an explosion of good luck.

The results are seldom so dramatic, of course. "Janice and I are just two people who seem to bring each other good luck," says Andrea, who is one-half of a New York destiny pair. Both are members of Alcoholics Anonymous. As is traditional in AA, they do not want their full names made public.

They met by chance at an AA gathering more than twenty years ago. Both at the time were down on their luck. Both were drinking heavily. Janice came from an affluent suburban background and had recently been floored by a painful divorce. Andrea was separated from a husband who was also an alcoholic but refused to seek help. When drunk he would turn up at her Brooklyn apartment and shout obscenities through the door until the neighbors complained and she had to let him in. These incessant visits upset her and kept her off balance. She had been through a succession of jobs, each one lower in pay and status than the one preceding it. "I was a mess," she recalls. "I had a quart-a-day drinking habit, and I was trying to support it by waitressing in scroungy restaurants. I was wondering if I could earn more money by prostitution. I was on the verge of a complete collapse."

Alcoholism and its control are both largely matters of luck, according to AA and other people who deal with it. "Of all men and women who ever start drinking, about 10 percent eventually became alcoholics," Loran Archer, deputy director of the National Institite of Alcohol Abuse and Alcoholism, says. "We don't know all the reasons, but we do know some. Genetics plays a part. If you're born of an alcoholic parent, you're a lot more likely to become an alcoholic yourself than somebody with two sober parents." The genes one inherits are of course beyond one's control and so would fit our definition of luck.

Whether an alcoholic defeats the problem is also dependent on luck. Of all those who ever turn up at an AA meeting, half drop out within three months and are never seen again. Of those who stick with it for a year, 41 percent are likely to make it at least through another year. What differentiates those who stay sober? There are many factors, but one of the most important—perhaps *the* most important—is the question of who else happens to be at the newcomer's first one or two meetings.

Mutual support, one member helping another, is the foundation of AA-style therapy. If you're an alcoholic and go to a meeting to see if there's help for you there, what happens to you will depend almost entirely on those you chance to meet. If you dislike them or find them too solicitous or not solicitous enough—if, for any reason, no spark of affection is struck—you will probably walk away forever, perhaps to your doom. But if you are luckier, you will meet people you can like and trust, and through them you may find your salvation.

And if you are really lucky, you will meet your destiny partner. It is not an uncommon AA story. It happened to Andrea and Janice.

"It was my first meeting," Andrea says. "I'd just lost my umpteenth job for showing up late. I was hung over and feeling terrible. Suicide was one thought that crossed my mind. I knew I needed some kind of help, but I didn't really think AA was going to be it. I just went to that meeting out of desperation. And by sheer luck, there was Janice. It wasn't her regular meeting place or time. She was there by a fluke."

Like Procter and Gamble, they formed a lifetime partnership that changed both their destinies. Janice helped Andrea sober up and stay that way. Once sober, Andrea was able to move back up the career ladder from which she had fallen. She found a secretarial job with the Prudential Insurance Company.

Then it was Andrea's turn to help Janice. After being sober for several months, Janice had a relapse. Andrea helped her recover from that and, then, helped her find a job at the insurance company. Janice had not worked at an outside-the-home job throughout her married life and would have had little chance of finding anything but minimum-wage work without Andrea's help.

Then it was Janice's turn again. By random luck, she was assigned to a boss who admired her skills and boosted her rapidly to a supervisory position. She pulled Andrea up after her. Soon both women were in high-paid, responsible jobs.

Then they decided on a joint venture. Pooling their savings and borrowing from a company credit union, Andrea and Janice bought a small resort hotel on the New Jersey shore. By paying special attention to the dining room, they changed it from just a summer business to a year-round attraction. It prospered, and they expanded their venture. Today they own and operate three small oceanfront hotels and have a half-interest in a shopping plaza.

Their business is not on the scale of Procter & Gamble, but they can be called unequivocally successful. It shows what destiny pairing can do. If these two women had not paired, it is hard to imagine what might have become of them separately.

A DESTINY PARTNER is more than just a friend. A friend is somebody you like and have fun with. The liking may even be profound enough to deserve the name love. But if this person doesn't objectively change the course of your life and the nature of your luck, then "friend" is the only right word.

Most friends are only friends. Some may be friends of very long standing: friends who go back to your school or college days, your old home neighborhood, good times long ago. Your heart warms when you see these people. But in terms of luck they are no different from anybody else in your acquaintanceship network. They may bring you isolated strokes of life-changing luck from time to time, but only a person who alters your luck over a long term may be called a destiny partner.

A spouse isn't necessarily a destiny partner either. It is sentimental and nice to talk about one's spouse in destiny-pair terms—"I could never have

156

made it without her"—but in objective fact, such statements may be true only in a limited sense.

It is certainly true that spouses affect each other's destinies by becoming linked economically. If one spouse achieves a high income, the other goes along for the ride. Moreover, they may change each other's lives by producing children. But in many marriages, that is about the size of it. The spouse who was going to become a great novelist or found a successful company would have done so anyway, married or not.

Such mutually noninfluential marriages aren't to be disparaged. The two spouses may love each other deeply. The sex may be great, the kids happy, the harmony unassailable. But to talk about these two people climbing toward their destiny together may be only a romantic fiction. It would be a fallacy to assume that every contentedly married couple is a destiny pair.

On the other hand, such married pairs do exist. In the theatrical world, Alfred Lunt and Lynn Fontaine were a destiny pair, for example. To a lesser degree, so were Humphrey Bogart and Lauren Bacall. Each had targeted his or her destiny before they met, but their forward motion seemed to be slowing and their luster was dimming. If they had not come together, both might have fallen separately to obscurity. By forming a partnership, they vastly increased the sum of their parts.

Some other examples are to be found among recent couples occupying the White House. John and Jacqueline Kennedy were probably a destiny pair. Richard and Pat Nixon were not. Ronald and Nancy Reagan may be, but that marriage is so fiercely private that we may never know for sure.

HOW DO YOU meet your destiny partner? It usually happens by blind luck, as it did in the case of Procter and Gamble, Andrea and Janice—not to mention any number of other famous destiny pairs such as Gilbert and Sullivan, Ginger Rogers and Fred Astaire, Samuel Johnson and James Boswell. That being so, the best way to boost your chances of meeting the person who will change your luck is to practice the Second Technique: Put yourself out in the fast flow.

In a few cases, destiny pairs meet in part because one goes looking for the other. Luck always plays a large role, but the active looking can make a lucky hit more likely. This could happen to you as either the seeker or the sought.

A classic case of this seeker-and-sought pairing is the story of Margaret Mitchell and Harold Latham. If these two had never met, it is probable that the world would never have heard of *Gone with the Wind.*

One of the most successful novels and movies in all history, this grand work owed its birth and maturing to a series of lucky flukes, culminating in the fluke of the Mitchell-Latham pairing. That was the kingpin fluke, the one that brought and held everything else together. Before it occurred, however, the author's life was pushed this way and that by a number of other events that were not of her making.

Margaret Munnerlyn Mitchell, who preferred to be called Peggy, wanted to be a doctor. She started college in 1918 with that goal in view. Then the first chancy event struck. A worldwide epidemic of flu took millions of lives in 1919, and among those lives was that of Peggy Mitchell's mother, back home in Atlanta, Georgia. Peggy went back there—temporarily, she thought—to keep house for her father.

After a while she made an attempt to resume her premedical college career, but she found herself homesick and distracted, unable to keep up with the academic competition. After nearly flunking some courses, she returned to Atlanta permanently.

She married, divorced, married again—the second time to advertising executive John Marsh. There were no children by either marriage. To absorb a restless energy that seemed to increase in each year of her twenties, she turned to sundry literary pursuits. She had always been an engaging, witty writer. She got a job as a newspaper feature reporter. She also became a familiar figure at parties and gatherings of Atlanta's young arty-intellectual set.

Then another chancy event nudged her life along a different course. The event this time was an automobile accident, the first of three in which she would be involved in her lifetime.

Margaret Mitchell had been accident-prone since childhood, and it would be an accident, finally, that would end her life. There are a lot of psychoanalytic theories about accident-proneness. Most are too goofy to take seriously. They are like those theories about compulsive gambling. Just as the compulsive gambler supposedly wants to lose, so the accident-prone person allegedly wants to get hurt or killed, to atone for some real or imagined sin. Perhaps it is so in some cases. In most, however, accident-proneness is a form of bad luck resulting from ordinary carelessness. It comes most often from a failure to apply the Eighth Technique: worst-case analysis. The accident-prone man or woman, far from being depressed and searching for punishment, tends to be overoptimistic, happy-go-lucky. He or she blunders trustingly into situations instead of saying "Now, wait a minute, how can this go wrong?"

Margaret Mitchell seems to have been one of these people. She had had at least two serious horseback riding accidents as a girl. Now, as a young woman of twenty-six, one year after her marriage to John Marsh, she had her first automobile accident. Driving alone in wet weather, she skidded off a road. Her ankle was injured severely enough to keep her virtually housebound for more than a year. As a result, she had to give up her reporting career.

So here was this young woman of lively intellect and restless energy, stuck in the house by herself. She had no children to absorb her attention. Nor was housework her cup of tea. What could she do? She started a novel.

It was the story of a woman named Pansy (later renamed Scarlett) O'Hara, whose character matures and hardens as she wrestles with a series of challenges during the Civil War. The novel was essentially finished in late 1929 or 1930. It was enormously and intimidatingly long, more than two thousand pages stuffed into envelopes and file folders.

It sat in those envelopes and folders, slowly turning yellow, for five or six years. Later, Margaret Mitchell maintained steadfastly that she never submitted the manuscript to anybody in all that time. Some say she did show at least some chapters to a few editors, but they rejected the novel;

and after those early attempts, she gave up trying to get it published. If that version is true, the editors involved can of course be counted on to keep quiet forever about their ghastly error of judgment.

Be that as it may, the great novel lay dormant, all but abandoned. For a time, parts of it were used to prop up a sofa—it was just so much paper. It needed a stroke of luck to bring it to life.

The luck came in the person of Margaret Mitchell's destiny partner, Harold Latham.

Latham was editor in chief and vice president of the Macmillan Company. In 1935, nine years after Margaret Mitchell had started writing her novel, he stopped off in Atlanta while on a tour of the South. Recent developments in the book business made him think the time was propitious for historical novels set in the South, and he was out looking for some. When he first got to Atlanta, he was disappointed. An advance scouting party was supposed to have lined up some promising authors for him to talk to but had failed to find any. He retired grumpily to his hotel room and made some phone calls. Luckily for Margaret Mitchell, she had always kept herself in the fast flow. Somebody knew somebody who knew her.

"Is she working on anything?" Latham asked.

"I heard her mention a novel years ago. I don't know."

Latham managed to meet Margaret Mitchell. She denied the existence of the supposed novel, perhaps because she was convinced by now that it was worthless. Still, she and Harold Latham did take to each other instantly.

They were a mismatched-looking pair. Latham was a big, blundering bear of a man with steel-rimmed glasses. Margaret Mitchell was tiny, less than five feet tall. She had a kind of prettiness that did not age well. In her twenties she had been arrestingly good-looking. In her midthirties, when Latham met her, she was developing an unnaturally big-eyed look. In her forties she would turn fat and jowly.

Latham pestered her about her alleged novel. She finally admitted such a thing existed but said it was incomplete, nowhere near ready for the light of day. Latham gave up. He went back to his hotel for supper, then went up to his room. He was planning to go to bed early and catch a morning train home to New York.

His phone rang. It was Margaret Mitchell. She said she had changed her mind. She was down in the hotel lobby with her manuscript.

Nobody has ever offered a satisfactory explanation of this sudden change of mind. One biographer, Anne Edwards, says it came about because a friend needled Margaret Mitchell about her "seriousness" as a writer. That sounds plausible. But it may be more plausible to speculate that the diminutive novelist recognized the rare chemistry that existed between herself and Harold Latham. She could show her novel to him and feel comfortable about it. He was her big chance. If she did not seize this chance, fate might not offer her another.

That is the way it is with destiny pairs. If your potential partner walks into your life—a person with whom you feel a quick, strong and positive reaction—don't let that person simply walk back out. At least keep the newborn relationship alive while you assess it and see where it might go, for such a chance might not come around again.

The rest of Margaret Mitchell's story is much like the story of lucky Charles Darrow and his Monopoly. *Gone with the Wind* was published on June 30, 1936—a monstrously fat book of more than one thousand pages, with a cover price of three dollars. Working together, Margaret Mitchell and Harold Latham had fashioned that impossibly bulky manuscript into a coherent story that gripped people and wouldn't let go. Success was instant and overwhelming. Three weeks after publication, there were 176,000 copies in print. Two months later the figure had reached 330,000. A year after publication the total was almost 1.5 million and still climbing. When David Selznick produced a movie based on the novel, it became the biggest success of his career, and it gloriously launched the career of actress Vivien Leigh. Both the novel and the movie are still earning money for people today.

The destiny pair, Mitchell and Latham, stayed together. He kept suggesting that she write another novel, but she never did. Perhaps she felt she could never match that stupendous creative act, and if so, she was probably right. A second novel would almost certainly have been a letdown. Latham may have harbored the same fear, for he did not push her to write a sequel. They continued to write to each other fondly, talked often by phone, visited from time to time. In August 1949, perhaps brooding over the wonder of what had happened to her, Margaret Mitchell was struck by a car while crossing an Atlanta street. She died a few days later. She was forty-nine.

And so Margaret Mitchell was lucky in some ways but not in others. That is usually the way it is. Indeed, it might even be true to say that is *always* the way it is.

# 16. Getting Lucky: Putting the Thirteen Techniques Together

If there is any single truth that a luck-seeker should comprehend above all others, it is that life is disorderly and cannot be lived successfully according to a plan. No matter how fine and flexible a plan one might devise, there will be times when the restless tides of life will make that plan unworkable. No matter what rules one might set up for oneself, there will be situations in which observance of those rules is difficult or just plain impossible.

And so it is with the thirteen techniques of lucky positioning. Don't expect to be able to apply all of them all the time. Life will inevitably back you into corners in which, against your will and judgment, you will find yourself violating one rule or another. Don't be upset about this. It is the way life is.

I never met anybody who practiced all thirteen techniques all the time. A consistently lucky person is somebody who practices most of them most of the time and, when breaking the rules, doesn't break them seriously. By contrast, unlucky people practice few of the techniques and tend to break the rules often and for long periods of time.

If you seek good luck, it should be your aim to become adept with all thirteen techniques. Keep them in mind all the time. Review them often.

But don't give up on yourself if you sometimes find yourself failing to act in the right way.

ALL THE WORLD'S major religions realized centuries ago that life cannot be lived in a straight line. Christians, Jews, Moslems, Hindus—all have codes of conduct that they try to live by. The codes are alike in some respects, unlike in others. But on one thing they agree: human life being what it is, perfection is all but impossible. Only saints ever achieve it. Even the least tolerant Islamic sects allow that mortals are bound to stray from time to time. In the final reckoning, religious leaders assure us, nobody will hold it against us if we fail to achieve perfection. What will count is how hard we try.

And so it is for the luck-seeker. It is unlikely that you will achieve total mastery of the thirteen techniques. But if you achieve even a moderately good degree of adeptness with them, you may be astounded by the results.

For it doesn't usually require a drastic change in anybody's life to change his or her luck. Sometimes, all that is required is application of a single technique that was previously being ignored.

It can happen, for instance, with the Third Technique, risk spooning. James Sullivan, a New York City employee, is one man who will vouch for the exciting possibilities inherent in this technique. He was approaching retirement when, for reasons that he could never explain satisfactorily later, the thought came to him one day that he hadn't been risking enough. He had been a combat infantryman in World War II, but since then his life had been unexciting and not especially lucky. The most money he had ever held in his hand was a city check for some $800 in accumulated back pay.

Then, out of the blue, on a day in May, he decided to place a bet on a horse. He and his wife had been out shopping. When the thought hit him, she was fully in favor of it. They found an office of New York's Offtrack Betting Corporation. A clerk had to explain the bets and procedures to them, since neither had ever been inside an OTB office before. One long-shot bet involved picking winners of four harness races at Yonkers Raceway. The cost of the bet was $3. As the Third Technique teaches, if an amount to be placed at risk is that trivial, you might as well go ahead and risk it.

Sullivan picked his winners by use of random numbers. The numbers he used were the last four digits of his Army serial number, 5683. As he explained later at an OTB press conference, this was as good a horse-picking system as any for him. He knew nothing about horses—indeed, had never in his life been to a harness racetrack.

He won $128,844. Lucky? Of course. But before he could enjoy the luck, he had to take the risk.

The Second Technique, fast-flow orientation, can also produce fast, startling results of that kind. If you have been keeping yourself hidden and then suddenly thrust yourself into the fast flow, your life can explode with serendipitous events.

Or consider the possibilities inherent in the Twelfth Technique, the juggling act. Until now, perhaps, you have been depending on only one activity or a limited few to bring you luck. Who knows what might happen if you double your range of interests in work and play?

ONE GOOD WAY to get started on luck improvement is to ask yourself which technique has been most notably lacking in your approach to life. If you consider yourself less lucky than you would like to be—which is presumably why you have been reading this book—then spend some time analyzing your life. What have you failed to do or not done right?

Almost everybody can identify some prominent failing—even those who consider themselves generally lucky. Ask yourself what your main problem with luck has been. Have you let lucky breaks pass you by through an unwillingness to take the zigzag path? Have you become mired in stagnant ventures because you didn't know how to practice luck selection? Have you let a potential destiny partner vanish over the horizon? Go down the list of techniques and try to identify the one or ones you most need to work on. And then concentrate your attention there.

A good exercise that you can prescribe for yourself over the coming year—it's not only useful but is also enjoyable—is to read or reread some of the world's great novels and plays with the thirteen techniques in mind.

Pay special attention to stories with unlucky outcomes. What technique or techniques could have produced a lucky outcome instead?

This is an exercise you were never taught in a high school or college English literature class. What you were taught back there, as we have noted before in this book, was to look for "tragic flaws." Tragedy, as taught in school and college, isn't supposed to have any connection with bad luck. But now you have an opportunity to revisit your favorite tales and look at them in a new way. Look for the workings of luck, good and bad. You will discover that many a character does have a kind of tragic flaw, but not precisely the kind your Eng. Lit. 101 professor was talking about. What brings a character to his or her doom, as often as not, is bad luck brought about by a persistent failure to apply one or two of the thirteen techniques.

*Dombey and Son* is my favorite Charles Dickens novel, for example. It is written in a minor key but avoids excessive sentimentality—which is unusual for Dickens. It is probably the best feminist novel ever written.

It is the story of a man, Dombey, who fails to apply the Sixth and Thirteenth Techniques: fails to follow a zigzag path and then alienates his destiny partner. Dombey runs a moderately prosperous importing business. He dreams of the day when his son will join him at the firm's helm. When the boy falls ill and dies, Dombey is devastated. He never realizes that his daughter Florence, a loving and solidly capable young woman, could be the "and Son" of the firm just as well as the boy could have—indeed, is in all respects the better qualified of the two.

Dombey allows bad luck to become worse luck. Hit by the bad luck of his son's death, he could have zigzagged his way out of it by discarding his original plan and staying alert for new opportunities. Instead, he keeps his gaze riveted on that one dead plan—the plan of turning the firm over to his son. The firm gradually dies of neglect. Florence, the destiny partner who could have solved all Dombey's problems, is never given the chance to try.

Another grand story with an excellent illustration of luck's workings is John P. Marquand's *Point of No Return*. It is a tale of the Fourth Technique, run cutting.

The hero of the novel is Charles Gray, a young man struggling up the executive ladder in a bank. Much of the story is a flashback to his memories of his father, John, whose tragic flaw was his inability or unwillingness to apply the Fourth Technique. John, an ineffectual dreamer, came into a modest inheritance in the mid-1920s and parlayed it into $350,000 in the soaring stock market of that period. His son urged him to cash at least some of his winnings out of the market before the run of luck ended, but John kept putting that off. When the run did end in the fall of 1929, John was wiped out instantly. He committed suicide.

Remembering this tragic event, Charles does a lot of thinking about luck—particularly the difficulty of abandoning runs before they have reached their peaks. He concludes that the most valuable rule in the conduct of his life will be what he calls "knowing when to stop"—what we call run cutting.

But of all the techniques, the one that stands out most starkly in works of fiction, particularly tragic works, is the Fifth. This, you'll recall, is the technique of luck selection—getting out of hard-luck ventures before they trap you. Thousands of plays, novels, movies, and TV dramas have been built on the theme of a character who fails to apply this technique. The result of this failure can be lifelong entrapment in bad luck. This gloomy outcome is, of course, rich in dramatic possibilities—which is why authors and playwrights love it so much.

We've looked at Anna Karenina before in the book. She can see early in her long affair with Count Vronsky that it can't work, but she is unwilling to abandon what she has invested in it; and the longer she stays, the bigger the investment gets. She finally has to escape by throwing herself under the wheels of a train. Emma, the heroine of Flaubert's *Madame Bovary,* lets herself get stuck in a similar hard-luck situation and finally has to seek the same escape. For a story of a man trapped in a love relationship that he could have abandoned easily when it first began to sour, read *Swann's Way,* the first volume of Proust's massive *Remembrance of Things Past.*

Fiction is also replete with situations in which bad luck cannot be discarded so easily. *Gone with the Wind* is a fine example. Scarlett O'Hara might have avoided all her problems by walking away from the hard-luck situation when it first presented itself to her. She might have sold the family plantation for a low price, swallowed the loss, taken the cash and gone off to seek better luck elsewhere. But that, of course, would not have been as easy to do as it is to say. That is often the dilemma of the Fifth Technique.

Reading such stories is instructive for the luck-seeker, for you can ask yourself, "How would I have avoided bad luck in this situation?" If I had been at Tara when Scarlett's adventure began and if she had asked my advice, I would have said, "Sell out fast." But others might feel that Scarlett's material and emotional investment in Tara was too big to abandon for an unknown future. The case illustrates the fact that some luck decisions are easier to arrive at than others. By testing your own reactions to such a situation in fiction, you can prepare yourself for a possible future time when you will be required to handle a similar dilemma in real life.

FINALLY, FICTION WILL help you think about the kind of luck that you can't do anything about.

No matter how well you practice the thirteen techniques, you can still be brought to your knees by cancer, shot by a burglar, or barbecued by a nuclear bomb.

Conversely, though you practice none of the techniques and have been leading a generally luckless life, you can still be hit unexpectedly by a bolt of good fortune from nowhere. Like the citizens of Spring Hill, Tennessee. They were sitting around in their houses, minding their own business, when General Motors suddenly announced in 1985 that it was going to build its giant new Saturn automobile plant in Spring Hill. The startled citizens found themselves sitting on a real-estate gold mine. The market value of some houses and plots of land tripled in a few weeks.

Nice? Yes.

What can you do about it? Nothing.

Luck happens whether we invite it to or not. Good luck and bad are always weaving themselves into human lives, leaving some people happy and others sad and others dead. The world of fiction teems with characters who are crippled or killed by disease, like Dombey's son—or who, conversely, are granted sudden good fortune without making any special luck-improvement efforts of their own. Critics often complain that such lucky and unlucky events spring from laziness on the author's part. It's true that it is easier to manipulate characters by blind luck than to construct elaborate plots in which their good or bad fates result from purposive human action. But are such luck-dominated outcomes unbelievable or untrue to real life? Does it strain credulity to read about Dombey's boy dying for no good reason? Not at all. That is exactly what real life is like.

Your own life was undoubtedly influenced by luck before you ever picked up this book, and luck would have gone on pushing you around no matter what you might have read or thought. But now you have the thirteen techniques at your command. Your relationship to luck from now on will be different.

You have no guarantees, as we've seen. What you do have is an edge. Good luck!

169